THE
ESTHER
ANOINTING

MICHELLE M^cCLAIN-WALTERS

CHARISMA
HOUSE

Most CHARISMA HOUSE BOOK GROUP products are available at special quantity discounts for bulk purchase for sales promotions, premiums, fund-raising, and educational needs. For details, write Charisma House Book Group, 600 Rinehart Road, Lake Mary, Florida 32746, or telephone (407) 333-0600.

THE ESTHER ANOINTING by Michelle McClain-Walters
Published by Charisma House
Charisma Media/Charisma House Book Group
600 Rinehart Road
Lake Mary, Florida 32746
www.charismahouse.com

This book or parts thereof may not be reproduced in any form, stored in a retrieval system, or transmitted in any form by any means—electronic, mechanical, photocopy, recording, or otherwise—without prior written permission of the publisher, except as provided by United States of America copyright law.

Unless otherwise noted, all Scripture quotations are from the New King James Version®. Copyright © 1982 by Thomas Nelson. Used by permission. All rights reserved.

Scripture quotations marked AMP are from the Amplified Bible. Copyright © 1954, 1958, 1962, 1964, 1965, 1987 by The Lockman Foundation. Used by permission.

Scripture quotations marked HCSB are taken from the Holman Christian Standard Bible®, Copyright © 1999, 2000, 2002, 2003, 2009 by Holman Bible Publishers. Used by permission. Holman Christian Standard Bible®, Holman CSB®, and HCSB® are federally registered trademarks of Holman Bible Publishers.

Scripture quotations marked KJV are from the King James Version of the Bible.

Scripture quotations marked NAS are from the New American Standard Bible, copyright © 1960, 1962, 1963, 1968, 1971, 1972, 1973, 1975, 1977, 1995 by The Lockman Foundation. Used by permission. (www.Lockman.org)

Scripture quotations marked NCV are taken from the New Century Version®. Copyright © 2005 by Thomas Nelson. Used by permission. All rights reserved.

Scripture quotations marked NEB are from the New English Bible. Copyright © 1961, 1970 by the Delegates of the Oxford University Press and the Syndics of the Cambridge University Press. Used by permission.

Scripture quotations marked NIV are taken from the Holy Bible, New International Version®, NIV®. Copyright © 1973, 1978, 1984, 2011 by Biblica, Inc.™ Used by permission of Zondervan. All rights reserved worldwide. www.zondervan.com The "NIV" and "New International Version" are trademarks registered in the United States Patent and Trademark Office by Biblica, Inc.™

Scripture quotations marked NLT are from the Holy Bible, New Living Translation, copyright © 1996, 2004, 2007. Used by permission of Tyndale House Publishers, Inc., Wheaton, IL 60189. All rights reserved.

Scripture quotations marked RSV are from the Revised Standard Version of the Bible. Copyright © 1946, 1952, 1971 by the Division of Christian Education of the National Council of the Churches of Christ in the USA. Used by permission.

*To my heavenly **King Jesus**, may my life be a sweet-smelling aroma in Your nostrils. Your love for me is amazing. I'm overwhelmed by Your scepter of favor that You continually extend to me. My God and King, I love You so much!*

*To my earthly king **Pastor Floyd A. Walters Jr.**, for such a time as this the Lord has brought us together to rule and reign in life. Thank you for all of your love and encouragement through this process. I love you, honey, and we've only just begun!*

CONTENTS

Introduction

YOU WERE MADE *for* MORE

CAN YOU IMAGINE an all-female army—women marching in complete synchronization with the cadence of the Holy Spirit—moving together in unity with distinction and dignity to advance the kingdom of God?

I believe that this is a season when the beauty and power of women will be on display. Decades of oppression will come to an end. Satan knows that when women discover their true identity in Christ, his evil kingdom will come to an abrupt end. I believe the body of Christ will see a manifestation of what Psalm 68:11 declares: "The Lord gives the command; the women who proclaim the good tidings are a great host" (NAS). A strategic time in human history is coming when God will give a command, and an army of women who proclaim the good news will arise in the earth.

Not at all like the feminist movement, this new breed of women will not attempt to carry out their mission copying the dress and behavior of men. No, quite the contrary. These women will be arrayed in the softest silk and elegant high heels. They will be armed with resolve, wisdom, and true discernment, understanding that the true enemy has been Satan and not men—or one another. They will embrace their femininity as being a blessing and gift from God. I believe that we are this new breed of women.

The devil has blurred the lines and devalued the power of being feminine. We don't have to hide our feminine qualities and compete with men to accomplish our purposes. We must develop a clear understanding of who God created us to be. We must get a clear vision of God's ideal and make His standards the standards by which we live. We can't buy into the lies that say male standards are the standards we must emulate to gain respect, fulfill our purposes, and find our identities in this society. Only Jesus has the key to our true identities.

God did not create women to do everything men can do. Equality does not mean sameness. Equality means each person is valued at the same level as another for their unique contribution. In fact, the very differences we have are our greatest strengths when recognized and used effectively instead of being at odds with one another. The Word of God clearly teaches us that men and women are meant to be partners in life—not just in marriage. When we come together in unity and mutually respect and depend on each other's unique gifts, we begin to express the complete image of God in the earth.

Men and women alike were created in God's image and likeness. Our society changes its expectations of us from generation to generation. This is why it must be His Word alone that we use to correct the distortions and devaluing of the differences between men and women. His Word for us does not change.

Women were created to express God's rule and reign in the feminine form. God has mantled women with the gift of leadership to influence and impact the world for good. God created women to be nurturers. We were designed to influence and inspire those in our sphere with godly wisdom and gentle encouragement. We are helpers. We support and champion dreams and visions.

Godly femininity is nonthreatening and does not seek to intimidate. Godly femininity is power under control.

FROM INFERIORITY TO INFLUENCE

There is a great move of the Holy Spirit among women. Women all over the world are feeling a passion welling up within their spirits that says, "I was made for more." God is liberating us to move from a place of inferiority, competition, and fear to a place of power, influence, and courage. No longer are we feeling the pressure to put on "fatigues" to impersonate the masculine, but we are being healed and delivered from tradition and religion that have held us captive for centuries.

The Lord is releasing His favor and grace upon us to fulfill His purposes in the earth. The question is: Will we submit to the process of being trained and commissioned to fulfill these purposes?

We are being called to use our gifts and talents to impact our society—to preach, teach, pray, prophesy, and deliver nations. God is empowering us to follow His ordained direction. We are arising and influencing the world in ways we have never done. Women are rising with a new level of determination, courage, and unwavering faith. With this newfound resolve, we must be prepared and positioned properly. We must examine how God wants to raise us up to influence the kingdom and the world. I believe the combination of prayer and action will be two major keys to women influencing their spheres of authority.

Women are some of the most valuable, untapped resources. We are God's secret weapons. Light is shining, and favor from God is being bestowed on women to be all that they can be. God is establishing godly women with authority and positioning them with influence that will bring freedom to societies throughout the earth. Godly, grace-filled women are being positioned to overthrow the plans of the enemies.

When I think of this supernatural shift God is causing in the lives of women, I think of my friend and colleague, councilwoman and apostle Kimberly Daniels. In her college days Apostle Kimberly was the fastest female sprinter in the nation. She then joined the military and became one of the fastest female sprinters around the world! Then her life took a turn, and she spiraled into a life on the streets. But God stepped in, and her destiny was reversed. What was meant for bad became one of her greatest assets in the kingdom: through this process of life being the fastest woman sprinter in the nation to living life on the street, Apostle Kimberly gained the ability to relate to people from all backgrounds. Through her ministry she shares her testimony globally and has led many to miraculous salvations, inner healing, and deliverance. She has a bachelor's degree in criminology, a master's degree in Christian education, and a doctorate in Christian counseling. But she didn't stop there.

In 2011 Apostle Kimberly was elected to the Jacksonville, Florida, City Council, receiving almost ninety-three thousand votes while managing her own campaign. She did in two months what her opponents who campaigned for two years could not do. Her election results were miraculous and historical. With both her church, Spoken Word Ministries, and her position on the city council, Apostle Kimberly is currently influencing her city in both the spiritual and political realms.[1] She is a modern-day example of the full manifestation of the Esther anointing.

WHAT IS THE ESTHER ANOINTING?

There is a pivotal time in Esther's story when her past and present converged and her anointing was pressed out and revealed. At that point of convergence was where God, the great apothecary, took all of the bitter and sweet experiences of Esther's life and crushed them together under the oil of the Holy Spirit to produce what I'm calling in this book "the Esther anointing."

The Esther anointing is a grace that is being bestowed upon women to influence the current culture for the purposes of the kingdom of God. The anointing of Esther is one of courage and righteous boldness exercised with great wisdom to confront injustice and deliver a generation from destruction. Modern-day Esthers will have a humble, grace-filled, teachable spirit acquired through submitting to the process of the Lord. Many of the modern-day Esthers have been in places of obscurity, seemingly hidden and forgotten by God. But suddenly they will be taken out of the comfort zone of life and placed in positions where they have to speak a new language, learn a new culture, and overcome gender prejudice.

God, in His infinite wisdom and uniquely designed school of the spirit, has been equipping them for such a time as this. He uses every crisis, every injustice, and every victory to work together for their good; they have been learning obedience from the things they have suffered. They have been serving the purposes of God in wilderness-like places, learning to submit to authority in order to become women of authority.

Bitterness will not be the undertone of this company of Esthers, as Song of Solomon 8:5 asks the question, "Who is this coming up from the wilderness leaning [and depending] upon her beloved?" These women will be motivated by the love of God, leaning on His strength and abilities. They will not be intimidated by natural laws or deterred by the opinions of men. The fear of the Lord and hatred for the enemy will be the driving forces of these Esthers.

Many of these women will demonstrate authentic beauty, embrace their identities, and manifest the power of God in feminine form. They will develop strategic, holy alliances with male mentors, as Esther did with Hegai and Mordecai, to demolish division and competition between men and women.

These modern-day Esthers will have an anointing to gather people around the purposes of God. They will understand the times and seasons of God. They will facilitate gatherings of fasting and prayer to plead for life before the courts of heaven and earth.

The anointing of Esther is one of influence, righteous

boldness, wisdom, femininity, and favor. This favor that modern-day Esthers will carry is not for selfish gain. They understand that God's favor is to be used for their assignments in the earth. It's by God's favor that they are able to bring forth granted petitions even by ungodly civil authorities. This favor causes policies, rules, regulations, and laws to be changed and reversed for the advantage of kingdom. (See Esther 8:5.)

ARE YOU a MODERN-DAY ESTHER?

Where are you today on your own journey? Are you discounting the significance of your life because you are a woman? Have you lost hope in seeing the promises of God fulfilled in your life? Maybe you are thinking there have been so many terrible things that have happened in your life that God could never use you. Maybe you've said to yourself, "I've made too many mistakes."

The entire framework of the Esther anointing is rooted in a reversal of destiny. The Esther story is an example of how at one crucial moment in history the covenant promises God had made were fulfilled, not by His miraculous intervention but through completely ordinary events. The Esther story could be your story. God will take ordinary events in your life to fulfill some extraordinary promises to you. The Book of Esther is full of hidden hope. It is the one book in the Bible that does not mention the name of God, yet the message of God's grace and redemption permeates each word. On the surface it appears as though God is absent, but Esther's story proves that He is always at work behind the scenes in our lives to cause us to walk in our destiny in the earth.

This book will discuss the ways God reveals destiny to His leading ladies who keep Him as their priority. It will identify character traits that you must develop in order to fulfill your destiny; lead you to know how, when, and where your unique gifts operate best; show you how to uncover and guard against snares that will keep you from boldly walking in your assignment; and give you the motivation and encouragement you need to move into a place of significance.

Like Esther, you will learn how to yield to the call on your life and submit to the Holy Spirit's purification process. Esther went through a season of preparation physically and spiritually. You will see how her respect for prayer and fasting made her the humble vessel God used to rescue individuals, turn circumstances, and deliver nations.

Esther was a woman of clear judgment, courage, and self-sacrifice. Esther was lifted from exile and poverty to being queen. She did not allow her background to determine what God could do with her future.

If you sense you have an Esther anointing bubbling up on the inside of you, join me in the pages of this book as we discover what you have been designed to influence.

The greatest thing that can happen to you in life, the greatest source of empowerment you can have, is when you discover your position in the prophetic unfolding plan of God. This will be your unique factor, what you are anointed to do. My prayer is that you get acquainted with your anointing and become more and more aware of what you are here to do.

DECLARATIONS and PRAYERS
to ACTIVATE the ESTHER ANOINTING

I **declare** in the name of Jesus that I will arise as a
  mighty woman of God from the depression and
  prostration in which circumstances have kept me—I
  will rise to a new life!

I **declare** that this is a season when old things are
  passing away and all things are being made new in
  my life. God is calling me to active duty in His heavenly army.

I **declare** that this is a time when the heavenly Father
  will make all of my God-given dreams and aspira-
  tions come to fruition.

I **declare** that this is my time and season to accomplish
  and live in God's ordained purpose and destiny.

I **declare** that I will arise from fear and embrace the
  courage of the Lord.

❧

Oh Lord, I thank You that You are an extraordi-
nary God who will accomplish extraordinary things
through me. I release myself from self-imposed limi-
tations. I break every limitation that the enemy has
placed upon my life. Lord, Your Word says, "Loose
thyself...O captive daughter of Zion" (Isa. 52:2,
KJV), and in the name of Jesus, I loose myself from
every limitation, barrier, obstruction, and demonic
mind-set that has kept me from meeting my full

potential. No longer will I be deceived and trapped by traditions and the opinions of men. I was created for greatness! I was created to be God's glory carrier throughout the earth.

I will arise and be radiant with the glory of the Lord. Let the glory of the Lord shine through me. I am a beaming lighthouse of hope for many who sit in gross darkness.

Lord, give me words of wisdom that will guide and influence many. I will not remain silent! I break every demonic conspiracy designed to keep me silent! I won't let past failures and disappointments keep me silent. I will open my mouth wide, and God will fill it.

God, give me ideas, insight, and concepts to bring deliverance to many. You have anointed me to impart grace to those in my sphere of influence. The words I speak will release life to a hurting generation.

I am not in this world by chance. I'm not in this decade by chance. I'm not reading this book by chance. I am a modern-day Esther! I stir up and activate the Esther anointing through prayer. I embrace my inner and outer beauty. I decree that the power of femininity is being awakened inside of me.

Chapter 1

TAKEN:
FROM TRAUMA *to* TRIUMPH

So it was, when the king's command and decree were heard, and when many young women were gathered at Shushan the citadel, under the custody of Hegai, that Esther also *was taken* to the king's palace, into the care of Hegai the custodian of the women.

—ESTHER 2:8,
emphasis added

I'M INTRIGUED BY the passive tense in the phrase "was taken" in the verse above. In fact, this verb can mean "taken by force." The word *taken* indicates to be fetched or acquired like property. The edict went out across the land, and the king's guard was dispatched to gather the young girls. One minute they were at home with their families; the next minute they were whisked away to the palace and placed in a harem. Their lives were suddenly interrupted. The Persian Empire didn't care whether parents had other plans for their daughters. Remember, "Resistance is futile; you must be assimilated."

It's easy to dismiss Esther as a lucky young woman who won the heart of a king. Most people view the story of Esther as one of romance, but I would like to offer a different view-point. Esther was a woman with a tragic background. Both of her parents had died, and she was adopted and cared for by her cousin Mordecai, who advised her to keep her Jewish identity a secret. In fact, to call the process of collecting the women a competition is a little misleading since none of the "contestants" would be going home afterward. These women were slaves, whose lives were not considered their own. The king wished to add to his collection of living dolls; those chosen would live in secluded splendor for the rest of their lives, even if they were only rarely taken out and played with. How is this romantic? This is more in line with modern-day sex trafficking than a beauty pageant.

Imagine if you were going about your day and suddenly a government official comes and, for all intents and pur-poses, snatches you off the street. Why? Because the king, who is known for killing people at a whim, wants a new wife since he banished the first one. The previous Queen Vashti refused to show herself before the king and his guests after he requested her presence so that he could show off her beauty. (See Esther 1.)

Allow me to personalize this story:

Esther, whose name to her family and kinsmen was Hadassah, was living at a time soon after the nation of Israel was conquered by Nebuchadnezzar of Babylon, who had then been conquered by the Persian Empire. While some of the Jews had been allowed to return to Jerusalem, Esther's family was part of a group that decided to stay in Persia. Within their modest, tight-knit communities, many of these families kept all the Jewish laws and traditions, similar to how they must have tried to live in Egypt in the time of Moses. This is part of what angered Haman and caused him to devise an evil plot to kill all the Jews in Persia. He did not like that they refused to assimilate into Persian culture.

But as a young girl, Esther's concerns were far more innocent. She may have had dreams of being the mother of the Messiah as many Jewish girls did. She was probably around the age that most Jewish girls got married, around twelve or thirteen. She was raised in the Jewish tradition and was taught about the one true God. She was a member of the Benjamite tribe, so the Law of Moses would have forbidden her to intermarry with other cultures. So when the edict went out and the soldiers came to collect Esther, she must have known her life was going to be very different.

Being in line to marry the king of an opposing, enemy nation was against everything she had been taught and raised to believe. I imagine that her plight was similar to that of Daniel, Shadrach, Meshach, and Abednego.

I can't begin to personalize the fear and despair this young girl must have felt being stripped from her family, knowing that she would be forced into behaviors or practices that went against her beliefs about marriage and maintaining sexual purity. Virginity was a single woman's honor. In this place, this palace, all of that would be stolen and violated. Can you imagine her pleading with God as she was captured and rushed off to the "house of women," begging Him for miraculous deliverance?

These occurrences in Esther's life were unfair. She was indeed a victim. But her story offers hope to all women who have faced traumatic, life-altering situations and trouble of any kind that God can work through fears and dangers to accomplish your destiny.

OUT of the ASHES

Have you ever felt as if your destiny has been taken? Maybe when the opposition seems unbeatable, you wonder if God cares. You may feel alone in the world with its suffering, injustice, and pain. You are not alone. God promises to never leave you or forsake you, nor does He send harm to come upon His daughters. There is a very real enemy who seeks to steal, kill, and destroy all your hope. He doesn't want you to know or even fulfill your destiny. He will do this by causing you to blame God for the evil that the enemy sends into your life. And let me go further than this; we have the power to choose as well. Do we continue to live as victims or do we take on the righteousness and salvation of Christ and live as victors?

What do you do when life becomes too tough? You may think: "What can I do with all my troubles and baggage to help anyone else? How could my life, reputation, comfort, and future be used to rescue others?"

Great faith often emerges out of desperation and anguish, and people who perform brave deeds always battle fear and inadequacy. The hand of God is at work in the lives of His people. Just as He used the circumstances in Esther's life, He can also use the decisions and actions in your life to providentially work out His divine plans and purposes for you.

We can trust in the Lord's sovereign care over every aspect of our lives. God is invisibly at work, making even life's greatest disappointments and tragedies a link in a chain of good things yet to come.

We cannot see the end of things from the middle, and we must walk by faith, not by sight. The Lord will bring a greater good, His perfect plan, out of all the frustration we feel and out of all the evil we experience. When all is said and done, God uses even injustice to fulfill His promises to us. God is present in every scene and in the movement of every event, until He ultimately and finally brings everything to a marvelous climax as He proves Himself Lord of His people.

Trauma is defined as a very difficult or unpleasant experience that causes someone to have mental or emotional problems usually for a long time. As you start to see yourself through God's eyes, you'll begin to sense the depth of His love for you—and the limitless beauty He's placed within you—although you have seen ashes before you've seen beauty. Let Him replace your emptiness and pain with His rich and deeply rooted love.

This is your moment to be healed and set free. The Lord will give you beauty for your ashes. Ashes refer to the adversities in life, and beauty refers to how the Lord can turn around those adversities that He may be glorified.

I want to declare to you, woman of God, that everything can be taken from you including your dignity, but the power to choose what attitude you have toward the traumatic events that have happened to you will never be taken away. Beyond the pain in life, there is always a silver lining and light at the end of the tunnel.

With the Odds Against You...

God is not limited by the same things that may limit us in our natural, everyday world. He operates beyond all limitations—past failures, lack of resources, poor upbringing. God takes whatever we have and applies His love and favor to it and lets it soar, causing you to excel in the most unlikely situations. Here's an example from a young woman who experienced this very thing:

> "The vision is for an appointed time." The passion to help, protect, and empower orphans and vulnerable children burned within me since I was a little girl. However, when I expressed my desire, family and friends thought I was strange and lived in a fairy tale world. But I never got discouraged. It was all I wanted in life. Nothing else I was doing in life could satisfy or replace this passion. It was what I felt I was born to do.
>
> The odds were against me. I knew no one who shared the same passion I had except for Mother Teresa. I had no resources, no money, and didn't know where to begin.
>
> Many years had passed, but during those years I never gave up hoping and dreaming. In 2003 I was invited to join a team on a mission trip to three countries in Africa with Apostle John Eckhardt (overseer of Crusaders Church and IMPACT Network). I visited Swaziland, Mozambique, and Zambia. While in Zambia, the Lord said to me that here is where I would feed His sheep. I was elated to hear this.
>
> After talking with some of the natives and hearing the plight of orphans and what I could do to help, I immediately began the process of becoming a non-governmental organization (NGO) to be called Daughters of Zion International. Every year after 2003 I would travel to Zambia, leaving my job in

Chicago on unpaid leave to stay in Zambia for three months so I could become familiar with the culture, establish relationships, and check up on the small projects we had begun.

From 2003 to 2009 through our Bare Necessities Project, we fed sixty-five families comprised of orphans and the grandmothers as guardians. There were over two hundred children benefitting from this program. We gave food, clothes, shoes, laundry detergent, and personal hygiene toiletries to these families every three months. The project ended as the grandmothers were empowered through mini-finance loans to start small businesses to continue providing for their families.

In 2008 I opened a school, Zion Academy, in one of the poorest communities in Zambia called Mtendere. This community is overpopulated with orphans and vulnerable children. Children were at risk of being abused because the only businesses that were operating were house bars and clubs. I couldn't bear seeing these children suffer like this.

Both the children and parents were happy the school opened. The children were fed two meals a day and were provided with uniforms and school supplies. For some, those two meals were the only meals they ate. They were able to learn and play in a safe environment. We even had to purchase school shoes for many of them because their parents had no income.

Unfortunately the school closed after two years because the landlord wanted more rent than what the property was worth and more than what my budget could afford. All was not lost. We brought uniforms and school supplies for the forty children that attended, and they went to government-funded schools.

December 2010 I transitioned to Zambia to live and to work full time with the ministry. Currently we are operating a home for little girls who are orphaned and have been abused or abandoned. We receive children who were infected by the HIV virus at birth and those who were severely malnourished. By the grace of God they are doing well and have recovered a great deal in health and spirit.

I am grateful to God for the love He has given me for the less fortunate. I am humbled and honored to be chosen for such a rewarding ministry. I am grateful for prayers and support we receive.

—SHANI BRITTON

DECLARATIONS and PRAYERS to HEAL TRAUMA and ACTIVATE a SPIRIT of TRIUMPH

I declare that my light has come. No longer will I sit in darkness, for the Lord is releasing heavenly revelation and illumination to me. My purpose is getting clearer.

I am a woman who has mental, emotional, and spiritual fortitude. New strength is arising within.

I choose to move forward in the face of trauma. I will sustain a sense of personal meaning in life. I will not be destroyed by the events that happen to me. I receive inner strength to overcome.

I declare that I will not let difficult or traumatic events define and derail my destiny. I will not allow a spirit of bitterness, hurt, and unforgiveness rule my life. I refuse to have a victim's mentality.

I am strong and able to withstand opposition. I will continue blessing and serving the Lord and others even in the midst of storms and crises.

I am the arrow of deliverance that the Lord is polishing to strategically shoot out from His quiver.

I am a woman who is able to bear up under pressure and adversity.

I am conspicuous, distinguished, outstanding, and pre-eminent. I will shine bright like a diamond for the King of glory.

❧

Lord, You are my refuge and my strength, my very present help in a time of adversity. I embrace Your healing and deliverance. You are the glory and the lifter of my head. The brightness of God's countenance is turned toward me. I am the apple of Your eye, and the favor and glory of the Lord will arise over me. Lord, clothe me in a mantle of dignity and strength. In Jesus's name, I pray. Amen.

Chapter 2

FAVOR *for* YOUR ASSIGNMENT

And the maiden pleased [Hegai] and obtained his favor. And
he speedily gave her the things for her purification and her
portion of food and the seven chosen maids to be given her
from the king's palace; and he removed her and her maids to
the best [apartment] in the harem.

—ESTHER 2:9, AMP

WE NEED THE favor of God to fulfill our assignments in the
earth. I believe that we are given favor according to the assignment God has placed on our lives. Favor mobilizes others
to help us in accomplishing our destiny plans and dreams.
When the spirit of favor is upon our lives, it compels people
to assist us in our assignment. The Lord is raising up women
who will have a spirit of favor upon their lives. This special
anointing is not for personal blessings only. The spirit of favor
will position you in places of influence to bring healing and
breakthrough to the generations. This anointing of favor is
designed to help you help others and extend the kingdom of
God here on earth. God is calling women who will function
as deliverers in the earth—women who will save someone
or something (especially a people or a cause) from danger.

Biblically, favor can be defined as "the friendly disposition from which kindly acts proceed to assist, to provide with special advantages, to receive preferential treatment."[1] Generally, favor means goodwill, acceptance, and the benefits flowing from these. It is also used interchangeably with mercy, grace, and kindness. Favor is that which helps man to achieve divine destiny and God-given assignments with minimum effort. Favor promotes you. It will take you to higher levels of success and service. It did for Esther.

One day she was an orphaned Jewish refugee. One year later she was crowned queen of Persia. God's favor caused Esther to gain the goodwill of everyone she met. Favor spared her of the unnecessary or needless labor and toiling. Favor made Esther's countenance or presence appealing and endearing to prospective vision helpers. Everyone who looked upon Esther favored her. Esther had something about her that caused everyone to "favor" her, from the king to the women in the harem who were competing against her for his attention and affections. Josephus the historian called it a "thread of grace." She had a winsomeness that caused people to be gathered toward her. Webster's Dictionary says winsomeness is "being pleasant, delightful, attractive in a sweet, engaging way." A person who is winsome draws you to them. Esther obtained favor with Hegai that caused her to be promoted to the head of the harem and be given all of the resources that she needed to win her position as queen. (There is another side to this that I will uncover in a later chapter.)

Favor will open doors that otherwise would be closed to you. It puts you into position for blessings and influence.

Favor will even cause those in competition with you to encourage and respect you. Favor is that which moves others to help and encourage you. Without favor, destiny fulfillment can suffer needless delay or abortion.

The SET TIME of FAVOR

> Thou shalt arise, and have mercy upon Zion: for the time to favour her, yea, the set time, is come.
> —PSALM 102:13, KJV

"To every thing there is a season, and a time to every purpose under the heaven" (Eccl. 3:1, KJV). This is the set time the Lord is releasing an anointing of favor in the land. The Lord is causing the hearts of kings of the land to extend the scepter of favor to modern-day Esthers. The scepter represents authority. God's favor causes policies, rules, regulations, and laws to be changed and reversed to your advantage. This anointing of favor will cause ungodly governmental officials to grant your kingdom petitions. This is an appointed time when oppression is being broken off the lives of many women worldwide.

Whenever the time of deliverance and reformation comes on the time clock of heaven for God's people, He anoints ordinary men and women with the spirit of favor. God's favor brings forth prominence and preferential treatment. By the spirit of favor, God will promote you to strategic, authoritative positions to accomplish kingdom mandates. God's favor brings forth promotion, even when you seem the least likely to receive it.

Joseph, Daniel, Esther, and Jesus were not only favored; they also grew in favor as they advanced from one stage of destiny fulfillment to the other. (See 1 Samuel 2:26; Luke 2:52.) We should both desire to receive the spirit of favor and to grow in it. We should pray to enjoy favor from both God and man.

The Lord is a sun and shield. He bestows favor and honor, and no good thing does He withhold from us (Ps. 84:11). Joseph was a man who walked upright before the Lord. The favor of God protected and preserved him from evil. Favor caused him to survive false accusations from Potiphar's wife. God surrounded and protected Joseph with favor like a shield (Ps. 5:12). The favor of God shielded him and kept him safe in prison. God spared his life so that he could be named as prime minister and save his family and the world from famine. When you live a life pleasing to God by obeying His will, you will find favor with Him. God will also give you favor with people.

Favor surrounded and protected Daniel as he slept in the lions' den. God's favor surrounded and protected Queen Esther as she approached the king unannounced. Favor caused Esther to be put in a triumphant position over her enemies. It will help you conquer and triumph over your foes. Because of divine favor Queen Esther was able to frustrate a wicked conspiracy to kill all the Jews in the Persian Empire. She saw Haman, the king's evil adviser, hanged on the same gallows built to murder her cousin, Mordecai. Esther found favor with the king and so did Mordecai.

The BENEFITS of FAVOR

We are the righteousness of God, and as the righteous we ought to expect God's divine favor! Psalm 5:12 teaches us,

"For You, O LORD, will bless the righteous; with favor You will surround him as with a shield." God's favor changes everything in the life of the righteous woman!

Here's what God's favor will do for you:

- God's favor will empower your dream to be fulfilled in impossible situations. Favor will cause supernatural increase and promotion (Gen. 39:21).

- God's favor brings forth restoration of everything that the enemy has stolen from you. The favor of God will initiate a great transference of wealth (Exod. 3:21; Joel 2:23–27).

- God's favor is intended for the life span of the believer not just for a short burst or isolated situations (Ps. 30:5).

- God's favor assures you of victory in any situation. The enemies of your destiny cannot triumph over you because of God being with you (Ps. 44:3).

- God's favor will cause you to be established in a prosperous business (Ps. 90:17, NIV).

- God's favor will cause those who stood against the fulfillment of the plans of God to honor you (Exod. 11:3).

- God's favor will cause you to inherit generational blessing, especially in land holdings (Deut. 33:23; 6:10–14).

- God's favor releases overcoming grace in the midst of seemingly greater impossibilities (Josh. 11:20).

+ God's favor will cause the yoke of poverty to be broken and cause retroactive payment of riches to be released in your life (Exod. 3:21).

+ God's favor will cause you to prosper in the world system (Exod. 12:36).

+ God's favor brings protection for you and your family from crisis and destruction. (Gen. 6:7–8, NIV).

+ God's favor causes the preservation of life and invokes His abiding presence (Job 10:12).

+ God's favor brings promotion, even when you seem the least likely to receive it (1 Sam. 16:22; Esther 2:7–9).

+ God's favor will cause men to give you the resources to accomplish your assignment (Esther 5:8).

+ God's favor brings forth prominence and preferential treatment (Esther 2:17).

+ God's favor will cause your leader to hear your words and brings forth granted petitions and requests (Esther 5:8).

+ God's favor causes policies, rules, regulations, and laws to be changed and reversed to your advantage (Esther 8:5).

WHAT BLOCKS the FAVOR of GOD in YOUR LIFE?

Throughout the Bible we see examples that show how people could not continue to walk in God's favor because of sin, pride, rebellion against the ways and instruction of God, and disobedience. It is no different for us today. The Bible says that "God resists the proud, but gives grace to the humble" (James 4:6).

As women anointed and called by God, we cannot afford to operate outside God's favor. We must understand the importance of our maintaining a quiet, gentle, submitted spirit. In the eyes of God this allows us to be trusted with high honor and favor in the kingdom. Esther carried with her a spirit of humility, submission, and obedience. Because of this she was favored by both man and God.

If we ever sense that we have fallen out of favor with God, we can be restored. We can seek the mercy and forgiveness of God by repenting of our sins before Him. We can humble ourselves before Him and once again receive His favor. (See Luke 15:11–32.)

> I entreated Your favor with my whole heart; be merciful to me according to Your word. I thought about my ways, and turned my feet to Your testimonies. I made haste, and did not delay to keep Your commandments.
> —PSALM 119:58–60

God is faithful and just and will forgive us and welcome us back into His favor with open arms.

The KEY of FAVOR

I want to share a story from a very special couple. They are apostles and prophets who serve alongside me through the Impact Network. They left everything they knew and gave away all they had to follow a promise from God that He would show them favor in their next assignment.

It had been a few years that my wife and I felt the Lord tugging at our hearts to relocate and plant a new church. Being a pastor's son, the expectation was for me to take over my father's church. I just knew the Lord was raising me up to be the successor of my father. To my surprise, God had another assignment for me. I remember being in the lower level of my house in Milwaukee, Wisconsin, and asking the Lord, "Where would you have us to go?" I heard the Lord say, "Look up!"

As I looked up, there was a box on the desk with my wife's portable hair dryer in it stating "Destination: Glendale, Arizona." I knew then that God was shifting us to a hot, dry region. Before he shifted us, I heard the Lord say, "Do you trust Me?" Immediately I answered, "Yes I trust you." Then He asked me again, "Do you trust Me?" I answered again, "Yes, Lord I trust You." Then He asked me a third time, "Do you trust Me?" This time I said to myself, "I must not be answering this correctly." So I looked up the word *trust* in the Amplified Bible and it said, "Trust (lean on, rely on, and be confident) in the Lord and do good; so shall you dwell in the land and feed surely on His faithfulness, and truly you shall be fed" (Ps. 37:3).

From that day forth the Lord began to deal with me about leaning on Him, relying on Him, and putting my full confidence in Him.

The Leave

So we began to pack up all of our stuff that we accumulated over the past four years in our home, and the Lord spoke to me and said, "Why are you packing all that stuff?" He said, "I asked you, 'Do you trust me?'" I said, "Yes, Lord, I trust you." He said, "Well, give away all your stuff."

Now I must admit, I felt like the rich young ruler whom Jesus told to sell all his stuff and give to the poor (Matt. 19:16–22). Even though I wasn't rich, it was still my stuff, and it was hard to give it all away.

So my wife and I purchased a one-way airline ticket to Glendale, Arizona. We took only three suitcases: one for as many clothes that I could fit, another for my wife, and the last one to share for our shoes. Now, for a woman to leave all her shoes, I had to make sure I was hearing from the Lord.

Not only was I leaving my stuff, family, and job, but God challenged me to leave a mind-set. He told me, "Before I shift you, I have to strip you of everything you think you need for ministry." God began to deal with me like Joseph in the Bible who was stripped of his cloak of favor and honor.

After leaving my father's church and the denomination I grew up in, I felt naked. These were things I honored and where I felt favored. But God said, "I'm going to show you my honor and my favor. Do you trust me with your life?"

The First Assignment

After our transition to Glendale, Arizona, God began to give me a vision and a heart for the city. We planted our church in the inner city of Glendale right across the street from City Hall. God began to speak through me to our congregation about opening the gates of your city for the King of glory to come in. City gates represent places of authority. It's important that you have the right people standing at the gates of your city.

God began to show us two gates that needed to be open to His rule: the spiritual gates (religious leaders of the city) and the political gate (city officials). That is when we knew that God had an agenda for our city. We knew that God wanted us to take our city for the kingdom of God, and these two types of authority needed to be open to what God wanted to do. So God said, "I'm going to give you a 'key' of favor to open up the political gate."

Our first assignment and strategy was to adopt a neighborhood. With a very small congregation, we cleaned up our neighborhood streets, raked leaves, cut grass, and repainted the addresses on the city's curbs. The city donated all the equipment we needed to help clean our city. This strategy caused the city to see we had a heart for our neighborhoods and started an ongoing relationship.

Prayerformation

The second gate was to open the leaders to citywide prayer. We started Prayerformation—"Transforming Our City Through Prayer." We asked all the leaders to come together once a month to pray specifically for the hot crime spots in our city. We invited the police department to come and map out all of the high-crime spots in the city. We assigned pastors and prayer teams to these areas and asked the commander of the police department to give us the current statistics of crime in those areas. He was able to measure our prayers by watching the stats go down by 20 percent since we started praying. After that the police department nominated me to be part of their advisory board called the Gateway Advisory Committee.

R.O.O.T.S.

God began to deal with me about the youth in our city. With budget cuts the city was forced to close down all of their recreation centers for the youth in the inner city. God began to give us favor with the city council and the parks and recreation department. They asked us what would we do with those buildings if we had them. I began to write a business plan for R.O.O.T.S., which stands for

- ✦ Reaching higher heights
- ✦ Overcoming impossibilities
- ✦ Obtaining success
- ✦ Teaching new models
- ✦ Supporting the next generation

The city told us they had to be fair, and so they released a request for proposal, and we had to bid against ministries and organizations that had thousands of people. Our church didn't have a hundred people. Then the Lord said, "I have given you this building but withdraw your bid." So I withdrew my name because I've learned to lean on Him, rely on Him, and put my full confidence in Him. The city wanted an organization to be able to sustain the utilities and pay rent.

After a year went by, the city approached me and said, "God works in mysterious ways. Which building do you want?"

The city allowed us to take over their fifty-two hundred-square feet facility for our R.O.O.T.S. program for the youth. They agreed to pay the utilities for us, and we have the facility rent free. They also gave us

a check to get started. Everything has been donated
to us, from paint, foosball tables, air hockey, and ping
pong tables to TVs and gaming systems. We now feed
over sixty-five children two meals a day through our
recreation center. The mayor came out to our open
house and supports us 100 percent.[2]

—EMMANUEL AND BELINDA ALLEN
BREAKTHROUGH LIFE CHURCH INC.

How is that for building your faith for how God will
grant His favor to you for accomplishing His assignments?

I want you to begin to claim and confess the favor of
God over your life. God ordained your life before you were
formed in your mother's womb. It is His desire to prosper
you in all that He has designed for you to accomplish. Just
like Emmanuel and Belinda, God is calling you out into
uncharted waters, and He will accompany you with His
favor. He will open doors and gateways and ways of access
into every place you need to be to show forth His glory in the
earth. Will you believe this with me? You will not be stopped
or hindered if you follow His lead and yield to His process.

DECLARATIONS and PRAYERS to
ACTIVATE the FAVOR of GOD
for YOUR ASSIGNMENT

I proclaim that this is the year of the favor of the Lord!
    This is the set time for the favor of the Lord to be
    manifested in my life.

I am growing in stature, wisdom is increasing, and
    favor is being multiplied to me.

Let the favor of the Lord open doors to my assignment that no man can shut.

I receive preferential treatment, goodwill, and advantages toward success in every area of my life.

Let the favor of the Lord surround me as a shield.

Let the spirit of favor compel men to assist me in my destiny.

The kings of the earth are extending the scepter of favor toward me, and I have all the financial resources to accomplish the purpose of God.

Leaders and heads of state show kind regards toward me. Their hearts are open to hear and grant my request.

I have favor with everyone assigned to my destiny.

I receive life and favor of the Most High God.

Scripture-based confession to release the favor of the Lord

There is no better way to express our faith in God than to say what His Word says. These Scripture-based confessions on favor are an example of how you can confess God's favor over your life:

+ God surrounds and protects me with favor like a shield (Ps. 5:12).

+ The Lord is a sun and shield. He bestows favor and honor, and no good thing does He withhold from me (Ps. 84:11).

+ I actively seek and live by God's wisdom; therefore, I am highly favored and esteemed in the sight of God and men (Prov. 3:1–4; 8:33–35).

+ God's favor brings promotion and causes me to increase daily (Esther 2:17; Ps. 75:6–7).

+ My enemies cannot triumph over me because the Lord has favored me (Ps. 41:11).

కడ

Lord, my prayer to You is for a time of favor. In Your abundant, faithful love, God, answer me with Your sure mercies. Lord, grant me favor in every situation assigned to restrict my purpose and hinder my advancement. Lord, cause every wicked device to be broken, but by Your goodness I obtain favor. Lord, I thank You for favor to complete my assignment in the earth. You are connecting me with key people who will unlock and advance Your purpose in my life. Lord, let my life carry the fragrance of favor. Lord, You are my sun and shield; You bestow upon me favor and honor. There is no good thing withheld from me. Lord, I thank You for supernatural increase and promotion. Let Your presence and Your care preserve and protect me. In Jesus's name, I pray. Amen.

Chapter 3

The POWER *of* YOUR PERFUME

Now when the turn of each maiden came to go in to King Ahasuerus, after the regulations for the women had been carried out for twelve months—since this was the regular period for their beauty treatments, six months with oil of myrrh and six months with sweet spices and perfumes and the things for the purifying of the women.

—ESTHER 2:12, AMP

ESTHER'S JOURNEY TO greatness and influence did not happen overnight. She did not arrive in the palace one day and the next day the king saw her, fell in love with her, and made her queen. No. She had to endure a beautifying process mandated by Persian culture. Every young girl in the harem had to go through this process before she could even approach the king. These special beauty treatments included six months in oil of myrrh and six months in spices and ointments. This process Esther endured has many spiritual principles that will help us understand the process we have to go through as God prepares us for our destinies and purposes.

The refining of our characters is very essential to God's plan for our lives. God cannot use a proud woman (or man).

Being taken through a preparation process presses and purges out impurities of the heart and spirit, such as pride, rebellion, selfishness, and bitterness, so that we can be pliable in the hands of the Lord to follow His lead to fulfill our purposes. We can't be an effective vessel with baggage weighing on us, affecting our ability to hear and obey God.

Beauty Preparations: Esther's Makeover

As we see from Scripture, Esther's beautification process involved two steps. The first step was very specific and lasted six months, involving only the oil of myrrh. The second six months isn't so clear. It just tells us that each girl had beauty treatment "with sweet spices and perfumes and the things for purifying." It doesn't give us a list of what those treatments or ingredients were. I believe God let us see it like this for a reason. I am going to break down both processes in the natural, step by step, then I am going to point you to the spiritual significance for all that Esther went through.

Stage 1: Six months with oil of myrrh

The King James Version uses the word *myrrh* with the reference to different plants. One of these was a small tree with bushy branches and three-sectioned leaves, bearing a plum-like fruit and producing a fragrant gum that had many uses. When myrrh oozed out of the bark of the bush, it looked like a gum resin that naturally flowed from the plant without any outside help stimulating the flow. It oozed out of the bush in the shape of a tear. The color of myrrh varies from pale reddish yellow to reddish brown or red.

There are many natural healing properties as well as

spiritual connotations to the oil of myrrh. Starting with the healing properties, myrrh does the following:

- Reduces inflammation
- Boosts immunity
- Speeds recovery from illnesses
- Eliminates respiratory ailments: congestion, colds, and coughs
- Improves arthritic conditions
- Reduces stomach gas and acid
- Fights fungal infections such as athlete's foot and ringworm
- Lessens menstrual issues
- Promotes oral hygiene
- Cures ulcers, gingivitis, and bad breath[1]

The word *myrrh* comes from Hebrew word *mara*, which means "bitterness." This process of soaking in myrrh was a bitter process. Myrrh is a unique ointment because not only is it used to purge, it is also used to preserve and as an embalming fluid. Myrrh was used in the making of perfume to preserve the fragrance. As a preservative, it kept things from rotting.

Without enduring the myrrh process in our lives, our fragrance would put off a foul odor. One of the foul odors that women should allow the oil of myrrh to purge from their lives is bitterness. I'm not saying all women are bitter, but I do believe it's a major assignment of the enemy against women. Hebrews 12:15 says:

> Exercise foresight and be on the watch to look [after one another], to see that no one falls back from and fails to secure God's grace (His unmerited favor and spiritual blessing), in order that no root of resentment (rancor, bitterness, or hatred) shoots forth and causes trouble and bitter torment, and the many become contaminated and defiled by it.
>
> —AMP

Bitterness is unfulfilled revenge. Its fruit is unforgiveness that develops into resentment. Resentment always wants to retaliate. In this world women have suffered cruelty, harshness, and brutality at the hands of thoughtless human beings. Our only hope is found in the Cross. We must forgive and release every offender. The Lord promises that vengeance is His and He will repay (Rom. 12:19). Every woman has a choice to remain bitter or to let it go and leave it to God to handle.

When a root of bitterness springs up, it not only destroys inner peace but it can also cause physical illness. Bitterness defiles all those it touches, starting with the one who is bitter and extending out to other relationships. Furthermore, the one embittered becomes enslaved to the person toward whom that bitterness is directed.

Moses gives us a prophetic picture of how we should respond to every bitter situation in our lives. The Israelites went three days without fresh water. When they finally found water, "they could not drink the waters of Marah, for they were bitter; therefore it was called Marah" (Exod. 15:22–23). The Lord, however, showed Moses a tree, and "when he cast it into the waters, the waters were made sweet" (Exod. 15:25). The tree that was applied to the bitter water was a picture of the cross of Christ. When we apply the Cross to our bitter experiences, it turns the bitter to sweet.

As Esther allowed the Persian attendants to transform and prepare her to meet with the king, we can imagine that their goal was to strip her of anything common or peasant-like. They wanted to purge her of her bitter past. I imagine that they hoped to infuse in her the scent and aura of royalty. You see, they gathered these girls from every part of the country. It doesn't say in Scripture that they had to be from a royal or aristocratic background. I imagine that, while these girls were physically beautiful, many of them were from common families and may not have known the ways of royal women. Therefore they had to be purified from their past lives as common, peasant girls and be infused with the scent of their new purpose as royal residents in the king's palace.

As we compare the health benefits and the possible way the ancient Persians used the oil of myrrh, we can see how the Holy Spirit purifies us and prepares us for royal service. As the Holy Spirit works in us, we will see the softening of our fallen nature, symbolic of soaking in myrrh. We will see that He will purge us of our pasts and put to death anything that does not line up with our royal destinies.

In ancient times myrrh was used to soften hard, dry, and cracked skin and restore its suppleness. As you can see, this softening is the work of the Holy Spirit in us. The anointing oil of the Holy Spirit is a beauty treatment for our hearts.

Stage 2: Six months with sweet spices, perfumes, and things for purification

> The ancient beauty process referred to as "six months with perfumes" has been illuminated by the archaeological find of a cosmetic burner from this period (Esth. 2:12). During the Persian period and even among some Arabian tribes in this century, women would build a small charcoal fire in a pit in the floor. A fragrant oil, such as that from sandalwood, cloves, myrrh, or rose, would be placed in the cosmetic burner and heated in the fire. The woman would crouch naked over the burner with her robe draped over her head and body to form a tent. As she perspired, her open pores absorbed the fragrance of the oil. By the time the fire burned out, her skin and clothing would be thoroughly perfumed. Aromatic oils and spices were Persia's major export.[2]

In the unsanitary and odor-laden ancient world, perfumes were highly prized. Perfume making, which included the preparation of both cosmetics and medical ointments, is an ancient and noble profession (Exod. 30:25, 35; 1 Sam. 8:13; Neh. 3:8). Perfume ingredients mentioned in the Bible included aloes, bdellium, calamus, cassia, cinnamon, frankincense, myrrh, nard, onycha, and saffron. Perfume came in the form of powders, liquids, incense, or ointments. Sachets of dried spices were worn under clothing (Song of Sol. 1:13), and liquids and ointments were contained in flasks and jars (Mark 14:3; Luke 7:37). Perfumed oils were used in these ways:

1. To soften the skin and mask unpleasant odors (Ruth 3:3; Ps. 45:8; Ezek. 16:9; Luke 7:38)

2. As an enticement to love-making (Esther 2:12; Prov. 7:17)

3. As a symbol of honor and hospitality to be poured over the feet or heads of banquet guests (Luke 7:46).

If you look again at Esther 2:12, you will notice that when describing the second six months of the young maidens' beauty regimen, the specific spices, oils, or herbs that were used to perfume them are not mentioned. I believe this is because each girl had a special scent customized specially for them. Each girl had a different body chemistry. Each girl had a different background. Each girl had a unique essence that was complemented and brought out by the perfect mixture design by the Persian apothecaries.

Even today perfume is made up of a combination of many things, but the process of infusing scents into our natural bodies is not as intricate as it was in Esther's time. But I believe this process still represents the time-consuming, delicate, and unique work the Holy Spirit does in us to cause us to exude a scent that is pleasing to God.

Like many of the girls taken into the king's palace, your background is the base with which God starts. Maybe you were a wildflower. Maybe you were a carefully manicured and sheltered rose. Whatever your beginnings were, God wants to take the hint of your scent, pair it with the oil of the Holy Spirit, and fill the atmosphere where you are.

Everyone has a unique fragrance in the earth. God is making women a fragrance. All of your life experiences—the good, the bad, and the ugly—blended together in right proportion produces your unique fragrance. Your life experiences, the Word of God that you've studied and made a part of your life, the encounters you've had with God, and obstacles you've overcome all make the fragrance. The perfume is equivalent to the life you have lived. God's nature is redemptive, and everything you've experienced in this life will be turned around for His glory.

The Fragrance of a Godly Woman

> Ointment and perfume delight the heart, and the sweetness of a man's friend gives delight by hearty counsel.
>
> —Proverbs 27:9

Women were made to manifest God in feminine form. We have a uniqueness. God designed us to respond to situations as He does. The way you respond to circumstances shapes you. Don't curse if they curse you. Realize that in a mud fight both people get dirty. God wants us to stay in our feminine nature. Esther was in an out-of-control situation, but she responded to it with grace and wisdom.

The body of Christ will not be complete until the scent of true and godly femininity can fill a room. In Proverbs 27:9 perfume and ointment are compared to a friend who gives godly insight and counsel. Counsel is to show a plan; it's to show a purpose.

Counsel and wisdom from the woman's point of view is needed in the church. Wise counsel from the feminine nature is needed in the atmosphere. Women with wise counsel add value. Women are called to make those around them see themselves in a better light. Perfume is all about influence. Your response to situations is the fragrance that fills a room.

Looking at Esther's attitude and actions in her situation, you will notice that her responses carried the fragrance of prudence, wisdom, and discretion.

Perfume bottles come in many beautiful shapes and creative designs. This represents the outer appearance of a woman. But we all know that you can have very beautiful bottles but bad perfume within the bottle. Have you ever purchased a very expensive bottle of perfume and when you got it home, the fragrance didn't mix with your body chemistry and it smelled terrible? This is how roots of bitterness defile a woman's fragrance. Her attitude and response to situations emit a foul odor causing many to be defiled by her odor.

Suffering does not automatically make a person stronger or better. The way you respond to suffering determines whether that hurt makes you better or bitter.

The fragrance of love

God wants to eliminate anger, bitterness, hatred of men, and unforgiveness from women's hearts. The only way to become better and not bitter is to extend love and forgiveness. But if you fail to react with love and forgiveness, if you retain in your spirit the debt the offender owes you, that offense will rob your heart of its capacity to love. Bitterness can have far-reaching, long-lasting, and self-destructive effects. A bitter woman must first turn to Christ (Rom. 5:8–10). Once she has accepted His forgiveness, then she is not only able but also commanded to forgive others (Matt. 6:15). One very practical way to do that is to replace bitterness with love (1 Cor. 13:4–7; Gal. 5:22), especially by showing love to the one who has wronged you. The memory of how you respond to life will become part of some other person's ingredient when it comes time for them to make their perfume. There are eyes always watching you, especially our young girls, to see what fragrance you leave behind.

Priceless Beauty

> Let not yours be the [merely] external adorning with [elaborate] interweaving and knotting of the hair, the wearing of jewelry, or changes of clothes; but let it be the inward adorning and beauty of the hidden person of the heart, with the incorruptible and unfading charm of a gentle and peaceful spirit, which [is not anxious or wrought up, but] is very precious in the sight of God.
>
> —1 Peter 3:3–4, AMP

Peter directs us to a priceless, authentic kind of beauty that should be more desirable than the beauty fashion magazines of our culture promise. Your beauty should not come from only outward adornment, such as braiding of the hair and the wearing of gold jewelry and fine clothes. Instead, it should be that of your inner character and personality and the unfading beauty of a gentle and quiet spirit, which is of great worth in God's sight.

Esther was a beautiful young woman, but her beauty was far more the just physical. Since all of the ladies were attractive, it could not have been Esther's physical beauty alone that won the king's affections. Her real beauty was an unfading beauty that rose from within. Such beauty does not rely on superficial helps; it's deeply rooted in faith and trust in God. No matter how many plastic surgeries you pay for, you cannot purchase this beauty—it's priceless. It's a beauty that is cultivated as our hearts respond in obedience to God's will for our lives.

I believe we can gain insight to the nature of Esther's personality by looking at her Jewish and Persian names. All through the Bible names have great significance. Names are connected to the nature and character of a person. Esther's Jewish name was *Hadassah*, meaning "myrtle." Myrtle is an aromatic tree, which is actually used in making some types of perfumes. It is known both for its scent and for its beauty. Esther was more than just another pretty face. Her personality radiated the fragrance of humility and elegance. The aroma of her personality caused everyone to become intoxicated in her presence. Esther exhibited a winsomeness that caused her to gain favor with everyone she came in contact with.

Esther, the Persian name given to Hadassah, means "star." A star is a fixed, luminous point in the night sky. The Lord was positioning and preparing Esther to be transformed into the nature of a star. She would become a beacon of hope in a dark time in her people's history. The characteristic of a star is to give light, guidance, and leadership. Another definition for the name Esther is "concealed and hidden." Esther demonstrated wisdom, prudence, and submission to authority by keeping her nationality a secret.

A soft and peaceful spirit, forgiving, kind, wise, insightful, discerning, humble, elegant, loving, and graceful are the elements to come together to form the beautiful fragrance of a godly woman. Esther personifies these attributes in her leadership and decision-making. Through her experiences we find a guide for how we can demonstrate the feminine side of God's character. Through Esther's story we are given a template for how women can engage the kingdom, sometimes dominated by men. The elements of the feminine spirit are complementary and significant to the expansion of God's kingdom.

Because of the sweet fragrance that Esther emitted, she was not only accepted by the king, but also she was favored by him and made his wife. Her influence was far reaching across both the Jewish and Persian cultures for years to come. Because Esther allowed the oil of the Holy Spirit to beautify and purify her, her legacy was chronicled in both Persian and Jewish history. According to one commentary, if it had not been for Esther's influence, Nehemiah may not have been able to rebuild the temple in Jerusalem.[3]

> And the king said unto me, (the queen also sitting by him,) For how long shall thy journey be? and when wilt thou return? So it pleased the king to send me; and I set him a time.
>
> —Nehemiah 2:6, kjv

> "…the queen also sitting by him"—As the Persian monarchs did not admit their wives to be present at their state festivals, this must have been a private occasion. The queen referred to was probably Esther, whose presence would tend greatly to embolden Nehemiah in stating his request; and through her influence, powerfully exerted, it may be supposed, also by her sympathy with the patriotic design, his petition was granted, to go as deputy governor of Judea, accompanied by a military guard, and invested with full powers to obtain materials for the building

in Jerusalem, as well as to get all requisite aid in promoting his enterprise.[4]

Like Esther, we too can have far-reaching influence and a
legacy that spans cultures and generations. We must submit
to the beautification and purification process of the Holy
Spirit. His refining will purge out of us the things that will
hinder us from being the women God has called us to be and
infuse into us the fragrant character of God. As we begin
to authentically display the attributes of a godly woman, we
will find favor for our assignments. We will find the scepter
being extended to us without limit to every place our feet
should tread.

PRAYER to ACTIVATE the BEAUTIFICATION PROCESS of the HOLY SPIRIT

*Lord, Your Word says that You will make every-
thing beautiful in its time. I submit my life and destiny to Your making and timing. I surrender all
ambition and striving to You. I ask that You will
give me grace to endure the purifying process. I realize that the race is not given to the swift or strong but
to the one who endures to the end.*

*I choose to submit to the inner dealings of the
Holy Spirit. Lord, remove anything from my heart
that will hinder my destiny. A broken and contrite
heart You will not despise. Cleanse me of all pride,
arrogance, and fear. Let love and kindness flow from
my heart.*

*The world has many definitions of beauty, but,
Lord, I want to radiate the authentic beauty of the*

kingdom. Favor can be deceitful and beauty vain, but a woman who fears the Lord, she will be praised. I am a woman who fears the Lord. I will develop traits of kindness and humility.

Lord, remove all mixture of the negative life experience from my behavior and values. I choose to be better and not bitter. Let the fire of the Holy Ghost purge away bitterness, anger, frustration, and disappointment.

I submit to the anointing of myrrh. Let the oil of myrrh cleanse every wrinkle and blemish in my character. I am a sweet-smelling fragrance and preservative in the rotting and decaying world around me. I will release the fragrance of joy, love, and hope to a dying world.

Thank You, God, for being faithful to completing this work in me. In Jesus's name, amen.

Chapter 4

AWAKEN *to* DESTINY

The high destiny of the individual is to serve rather than
to rule.[1]

—ALBERT EINSTEIN

"I F I PERISH, I perish" (Esther 4:16). What a statement of
resolve and courage. This statement of Esther reflects an
internal awakening to her purpose and destiny. Her declaration came after her cousin Mordecai asked her to go to the
king and petition for her people's lives. Mordecai had learned
of a plot schemed by Haman, one of the king's top officials at
the time, to kill off all the Jews in the kingdom because they
did not live by the rules of King Xerxes's kingdom. Like the
wise man that he was, Mordecai went further to point out
that all of the previous circumstances of Esther's life that led
her to the Persian throne may have been just for this moment
when she could intercede for her people:

> Do not think in your heart that you will escape in the
> king's palace any more than all the other Jews. For if
> you remain completely silent at this time, relief and
> deliverance will arise for the Jews from another place,
> but you and your father's house will perish. Yet who

> knows whether you have come to the kingdom for
> such a time as this?
>
> —ESTHER 4:13–14

Many times I've taught that we don't decide our destiny; we discover it. When destiny comes knocking on our doors, we may not often recognize it because it's not glamorous, it involves some death to self, and it always involves people other than us.

The moment of truth had arrived for Esther. She had a clear and life-changing choice to make. Would she continue to live in obscurity caught in the politics of two worlds, or would she step up to the plate and dictate decisive action on behalf of her people?

You must understand that this was not as easy as one, two, and three for Esther. This was not the direction her life was going up to this point. She was a young girl orphaned and living in a small town with her cousin Mordecai, when she hears that the king was searching for a new wife and she had to be one of the candidates. Esther was taken from her home and commanded to live in the palace, undergo twelve months of beauty treatments, and spend one night with the king to see if he would like her enough to make her his queen. Because of God's favor, she was pleasing to the king, and he chose her for his wife. I am summarizing this here, because we have to get into Esther's head a little bit to understand things from her perspective. She was practically a sheltered girl who now had the future of her people resting on her shoulders.

At the point that Mordecai comes to Esther with the request to go to the king and ask for her people's lives to be spared, she had been known as Esther, Queen of Persia. She had hidden her Jewish identity. Her birth name wasn't even Esther; it was Hadassah. If this secret got out, it could literally cost her her life. Esther had been living in a pagan society, adhering to laws and rules that governed the culture, and her life seemed to be controlled by her circumstances. She had been going with the flow, not rocking the boat, and not initiating action. Then comes this evil decree perpetuated by a wicked man.

The decree to have all Jewish people exterminated was a turning point in Esther's life. Would she cower in fear and continue to be a powerless victim of circumstances or would she be true to herself and her people and exercise boldness and courage to become an instrument of deliverance in the hand of God?

The choice Esther made at this crossroad became her defining moment. A defining moment is an occurrence that typifies or determines all related events that follow. The defining moment for Esther was a point at which her essential nature and character was revealed or identified. She had to choose between revealing the Jewish roots she had successfully hidden until now or stepping out and owning who she really was.

But could God really use her? She hadn't been living as a Jew. She hadn't been following the custom and manners of her people. I imagine she must have felt so inadequate. The decision she faced would define her future and determine the destiny of her people. It is only after hearing Mordecai's challenge in Esther 4:13–14 that Esther decides to act as

Mordecai wishes: go to the king unannounced, which by the way is against the law, and plead for the life of her people.

This was indeed Esther's defining moment—a monumental decision. It was an act of her will. She wasn't forced. She surveyed the situation, evaluated all of the teaching, training, treatment, and favor given her. And when posed with the challenge from her mentor Mordecai, she made the bold statement, "I will go."

What would cause a Jewish orphan, a virtual nonentity, to lay down her life for others? I believe she had an awakening to the call of God. Only a call from God would motivate a person to say, "If I perish, I perish." Esther did not have to sacrifice herself in this way. She was queen now; she had many privileges and comforts. Why should she give that all up? Esther was compelled to risk her life. This divine drive came from a place of her personal conviction that she was placed in the position of queen by the providence of God to save her people from total annihilation.

The MOMENTS THAT WILL DEFINE YOUR DESTINY

Esther 4:16 reveals a crossroad we must all face. Would Esther respond to the call of God to do something significant in history? This was a time when Esther had to make the decision to follow the purpose of God or cower in fear. The choice she would make would affect not only her life but also the lives of many others.

Our destinies many times are shaped by our choices.

Like Esther, your defining moment will represent your true self. You'll feel inspired to accomplish something greater than yourself. You may even think back through your entire life's journey that led up to your defining moment. Like Esther, you may have a defining moment that will lead you to a breakthrough in your identity. Take the time and look for those "little" things that have occurred in your life. If you look closely enough, you'll find that one defining moment, that one signature moment in your life when you realize how magnificent and brilliant you really are and that you are important and do matter in this world. You will be able to identify how the choices you make can have a great effect on the lives of many.

God is awakening many women today to a purpose greater than themselves. He is calling us from a mundane existence to a place of significance and fulfillment. Many women in the body of Christ have been trapped by tradition and locked into captivity by cultural and gender prejudice. Esther had to overcome many obstacles in her life to embrace and respond to the call of God on her life.

To be awakened has the connotation that you collect your faculties. You arise from a place of obscurity, indifference, and inactivity. It also means to rise up and take a stand, to appear, to produce, to be revived from ruins. The general concept of awakening captures the notion of either rousing oneself or being aroused in order to take action, as in the call of Esther. Such call to action is usually accompanied by urgency and intensity. It also suggests an arousal from passivity or indifference.

The sign that you are being awakened is that movement starts happening in your heart for an assignment. Questions begin to arise in your heart such as, "Why on earth was I born?" "Is there something more to the Christian life than what I'm experiencing?" "Could God in some way use my life to make a difference?" Here are some signs that you have had a real awakening:

+ You continually hear the voice of God in the area of awakening.

+ You have a divine sense of urgency and compassion for a situation.

+ You have a lamentation, that is, you have a feeling of emotional longing or pain for what could be or should be. A lamentation will make you put yourself in danger to resolve that issue.

+ You have the burden of the Lord, which is when a heavy weight comes upon you in the spirit to carry throughout the earth until the task is complete.

+ You have a priority change. Your life will no longer be about self-preservation but fulfilling the purpose of God.

In this time of awakening Esther lamented the future of her people. She knew that if she stood in the gap and acted on their behalf, she could be put to death. But this did not stop her from pursuing justice on their behalf. It would seem that because she carried the title of queen that she could step in and rewrite the edict against her people. However, it was only after she accepted her destiny that she could operate in her full authority as queen. And it is only then that she was referred to as Queen Esther.

YOUR CHOICES SHAPE YOUR DESTINY

I call heaven and earth to record this day against you,
that I have set before you life and death, blessing and
cursing: therefore *choose* life, that both thou and thy
seed may live.
                                    —DEUTERONOMY 30:19, KJV,
                                                    emphasis added

As I have already mentioned, Esther was faced with a
choice to step out of her comfort zone and exercise her
authority as queen to save her people or stand idly by and
watch them perish. She arrived at this crossroad just as
Mordecai revealed to her the evil plot set up by Haman. She
had a life-and-death choice to make that would determine
her and her people's destiny. It is now defined in history by
the choice she made to rescue her people at any cost. She is
known as a heroine, a woman of great courage and bravery, a
woman of influence. How you wish to be known depends on
you making the right choices at the right time in some of the
most difficult circumstances.

Choice plays a major part in fulfilling destiny. Choice is an
act of selecting or making a decision when faced with two or
more possibilities. It is the power, right, or liberty to choose.
Choice is option. A decision is a choice that you make after
thinking about it. A decision is a determination arrived at
after consideration. It is a conclusion or resolution reached
after consideration. It's actually in your times of decision
that destiny is shaped. Choices make the difference in our
lives. Making simple good choices daily in our lives can lead
to great accomplishments.

The Lord has given mankind a beautiful gift in the dignity

of choice. When making a decision, you must always begin with the heart and mind of God. You must start with what is right according to the principles of the kingdom and not what is acceptable. We will talk about this more in a later chapter, but this is why Esther, her handmaidens, and the Jewish people prayed and fasted for three days. She needed to know the heart and mind of God and line up with it so that His destiny for her would be fulfilled. How else would she have known? How else will you know?

Thinking back on your prayer times, what have you heard God calling you to do? What situations has He called you to address? What problems has He anointed you to solve?

When making choices, we must consider our values because values impact our decision-making. Values are something that we believe in so much that they guide our behavior. Values help determine how we weigh the consequences of choosing one option or another. To make the right choices, our values need to be aligned with God's values. We need the wisdom, integrity, and will to make the right choices for ourselves.

Esther's choice to take a road less traveled yielded significant results. God has given us the beauty of choice to make decisions and tap into the pure potential around us. We must create structure by choosing, and God will breathe life into our decisions. Our lives are nothing but the result of collective choices we have made along the way. We must take responsibility for our choices instead of letting others and circumstances shape our lives. Take action toward your own progress, which most of the time is the righteous, hard choice, and sadly few people are willing to pay the price to accomplish.

FOR SUCH A TIME AS THIS

Mordecai challenged Esther to awaken from her assimilation into the Persian culture to remember her true identity. The statement suggests he was aware that God was working out His purposes: "Who knows whether you have come to the kingdom for such a time as this?" he asked his cousin (Esther 4:13). Who knows? Mordecai could not be certain, but he was proposing the idea that the remarkable turn of events in Esther's life—becoming the queen of Persia—had not come about by accident. She was placed in a strategic position at a timely moment to carry out a purpose. Whose purpose? Mordecai does not say, but the fact that he and Esther were Jews makes it plain that the Lord's hand was behind it all.

Like Mordecai and Esther, you may face circumstances about which you have little if any insight. Whether or not Scripture is silent on the issue, you may wonder what God is up to. What does it all mean? In moments like these you can engage in the kind of reflection that Mordecai practiced— comparing the events of life with what you know about God to suggest what His purposes might be. The same God who worked through Esther is at work in your life today. Who knows what circumstances He might bring you into "for such a time as this."

Some defining moments may come unexpectedly and pass quickly, yet with far-reaching consequences. I believe one decision to obey God could change the course of your life.

If you know you have strong gift in a certain area, you

want to make a mark, and you want to leave the world better. But you won't know your legacy, even your greatest mistake, until years later. The defining moment will happen when you don't know it is happening. So the problem/challenge for us is we don't know the one thing we will do to make the biggest difference.

Esther had to choose whether she would stay indifferent to the plight of her people or risk losing her life. Had Esther developed a lack of interest or concern? Had she assimilated into Persian culture so much that she no longer identified with her Jewish roots? Maybe her new life had caused her to disconnect with her people or maybe she had lost her identity.

This is the struggle many Christian women face. Will we stay comfortable in our pews or will we rise up, engage our culture, and see positive change for the kingdom of God? One of the major spirits we must be delivered from is the spirit of indifference. Indifference causes apathy, complacency, and lack of concern to silently harden our hearts. We can become numb to the plight of others. Many times this happens because we've been rejected or pushed to the background by religious spirits in the church. We can develop a sense of feeling unimportant, insignificant, and irrelevant to the plans and purposes of God. Then there are other women who have been waiting so long to be validated and approved by authority that their hope has been deferred and their hearts are sick. Then there are others who lose their identities because they want to do what's acceptable to the masses.

But the Lord is releasing the sword of deliverance to break every chain that has held women captive. Women are receiving their identities from the heavenly Father. He is aligning our hearts with His heart. There is an awakening, an empowering, and validation coming from the heavenly Father to women.

BREAKING the CONSPIRACY of SILENCE

In Esther 4:14 Mordecai admonished Esther not to yield to the fear that would make her keep silent. *Silence* in this passage also means "concealed." Women have been told for years by religion to keep silent. But the Lord has given women a voice in every area of society. It's time to speak up and give a feminine response to life's situations.

Esther takes on a leadership role when needed by her people. Esther, frequently referred to in the book as queen, takes on the mantle of leadership at the turning point in Esther 4:12–16. Through her courage and willingness to risk her life, through her adaptation to her circumstances, her single-mindedness, and her grasp of leadership, Esther saves both her family and her people.

How many times have we said, "This is not a good time, Lord"? We can identify with Esther. The king had not asked for her in over thirty days. Maybe she had lost favor with him. But she still awakened to the challenge, realizing if not her, then who? If not now, then when?

Esther knew, just like we know: God works in His own time and season.

Esther got her timing right.

Maybe God has put it on your heart to do something for Him. Don't just jump into it but wait for His time. Joseph was in jail until it was God's time for him to be released. God will move in His time when we remain faithful and alert to His leading.

DECLARATIONS and PRAYERS to AWAKEN YOU to YOUR DESTINY

I **will** awaken from sleep and slumber.

I **will** awaken from complacency and indifference.

I **am** an active member in the army of the Lord.

I **will** engage the culture with my prayer and actions.

I **loose** confusion into every plan and demonic conspiracy to keep me silent.

I **will** arise and let my voice be heard.

I **will** preach Your Word.

I **will** encourage the next generation of godly women.

Let **every** dormant gift, talent, and anointing be awakened inside of me.

Let **every** God-given idea be awakened, activated, cultivated, and implemented for kingdom advancement.

I **will** answer the call of God.

I **will** not cower back in fear.

I **loose** myself from insecurity and fear of failure.

I **break** every religious spirit that has pushed me to the background.

I **shake** myself free from apathy and a lack of concern.

I will redeem the time in my life.

I will not allow a lazy, slothful spirit to control my life.

I will walk circumspectly, not as a foolish, silly, gullible woman. I am wise and know what the will of the Lord is for my life.

The Lord will redeem all lost time and restore every wasted year.

I will capitalize on every appropriate opportunity to fulfill my destiny.

I am a woman filled with the Holy Spirit.

My heart is experiencing a great awakening to my purpose and destiny.

I will seek and find the God who calls me.

I have vision and insight into the heart and mind of God.

There is a new level of urgency and passion for purpose arising in my heart.

I am significant.

I loose myself from hopelessness and despondency.

The Lord validates me, and He has called me and anointed me for such a time as this.

I will use my life and resources to accomplish great things for the Lord.

Prayer to Activate the Power of Choice

Lord, Your Word says in Deuteronomy 30:19, "I call heaven and earth as witnesses today against you, that I have set before you life and death, blessing and cursing; therefore choose life, that both you and your descendants may live."

Lord, I choose life. I choose blessings. I ask that You would give me the ability to make sound decisions. Let wisdom and discretion rest upon me. I choose to follow Your plans and purpose for my life. I choose to step out of my comfort zone and obey Your will for my life.

I will not be a victim of circumstance. I choose to forgive every man that has withheld promotions from me because I am a woman. I will not let a spirit of hatred of men infiltrate my heart. I will not let revenge, anger, and retaliation contaminate my spirit.

I will make godly choices motivated by love. I will walk in righteousness. I choose to be a woman of holiness. I choose to break out of the status quo. I choose to be a blessing to the next generation. I will leave a legacy of goodness and mercy in the earth. I draw a line in the spirit and choose life that my bloodline will be blessed. Because of my righteous choice, my descendants will inherit the earth. In Jesus's name I pray. Amen.

Chapter 5

RULE *and* REIGN WITH *the* SCEPTER *of* PRAYER *and* FASTING

"Go, gather all the Jews who are present in Shushan, and *fast for me*; neither eat nor drink for three days, night or day. *My maids and I will fast likewise.* And so I will go to the king, which is against the law; and if I perish, I perish!" So Mordecai went his way and did according to all that Esther commanded him.

—ESTHER 4:16–17,
emphasis added

However, this kind does not go out except by prayer and fasting.

—MATTHEW 17:21

ESTHER DEMONSTRATES MATURITY and wisdom in declaring a fast. She didn't operate in presumption. She knew that this was a situation beyond her control and only a breaking in the spirit and a strategy from on high would bring the deliverance her people needed. Esther commanded a fast for all those within her sphere of influence. She knew the power of unity. She knew the power that a quiet and submitted spirit would have over the enemy. She knew that her God would give her grace in exchange for her humility. Therefore for three days Esther waited in the presence of God to receive revelation from Him for the best course of action.

Calling a fast for three days implies that during this time of fasting, she would also be waiting on her Lord in prayer. That's what fasting is all about. The Jews didn't stop eating to lose weight; they fasted for spiritual reasons. When an issue this prominent became their concern, things got pretty intense as they filled the time they would normally spend preparing and consuming food in protracted periods of prayer and quiet fasting.

Fasting is one of the spiritual disciplines God has established to achieve breakthrough in our lives and in the lives of others. Before we attempt to do great things for the Lord, we should take out time to fast.

> Is this not the fast that I have chosen: to loose the bonds of wickedness, to undo the heavy burdens, to let the oppressed go free, and that you break every yoke?
>
> —ISAIAH 58:6

The scripture states that fasting will loose bonds of wickedness in our lives.

+ Fasting strengthens the spirit. (See Luke 4:14, 18.)

+ Fasting releases power in intercession.

+ Fasting releases direction for decisions. (See Judges 20:26–28.)

+ Fasting softens the heart and readies it for repentance.

+ Fasting breaks pride and brings humility. (See Psalm 35:13.)

+ Fasting releases strategy and breakthrough in a crisis. (See Ezra 8:21, 31.)

+ Fasting releases revelation from God. (See Isaiah 58:11.)

+ Fasting releases the manifold wisdom of God.

PRAYER and FASTING RELEASE the MANIFOLD WISDOM of GOD

Does not wisdom cry out, and understanding lift up her voice? She takes her stand on the top of the high hill, beside the way, where the paths meet. She cries out by the gates, at the entry of the city, at the entrance of the doors:

"To you, O men, I call, and my voice is to the sons of men. O you simple ones, understand prudence, and you fools, be of an understanding heart. Listen, for I will speak of excellent things, and from the opening of my lips will come right things; for my mouth will speak truth; wickedness is an abomination to my lips.

All the words of my mouth are with righteousness; nothing crooked or perverse is in them. They are all plain to him who understands, and right to those who find knowledge. Receive my instruction, and not silver, and knowledge rather than choice gold; for wisdom is better than rubies, and all the things one may desire cannot be compared with her.

"I, wisdom, dwell with prudence, and find out knowledge and discretion. The fear of the LORD is to hate evil; pride and arrogance and the evil way and the perverse mouth I hate. Counsel is mine, and sound wisdom; I am understanding, I have strength. By me kings reign, and rulers decree justice.

—Proverbs 8:1–15

I want to spend some time discussing the last benefit of fasting that I listed above. God is releasing a supernatural impartation of His manifold wisdom upon women. I love that wisdom is personified as a woman in Proverbs 8.

The manifold wisdom of God has many different parts and forms of expression. This speaks of the beauty and diversity of God's grace released to women. Wisdom is the process of discernment in which choices are weighed and alternatives judged. Wisdom is skillfulness. It is the ability to use knowledge correctly.

The manifold wisdom of God is applied in a special way to the many influential relationships that women have: wife/husband, mother/child, mother/daughter, and friend/friend. For the godly woman, choices are always to be made in keeping with God's purposes and desires. Let's go deeper into the expressions or virtues we see displayed above in Proverbs 8.

+ Prudence—acting with and showing care with thought for the future; to be mindful and careful of consequences of any measures and actions. Esther demonstrated prudence when she called for the people of God to fast with her before she went before the king. Esther took time and acted with care and thought for the future before she asked for what she wanted from the king.

+ Instruction—to teach by discipline.

+ Understanding—conveys the idea of learning through the unhappy experience of others; to know or comprehend the problem. Mordecai requested that Hathach explain to Esther the decree. She then made her decision to go before the king based on understanding and not just emotion.

+ Knowledge—is information of sound character. Esther used her knowledge of palace protocol to approach the king. She understood the culture and prepared a banquet for the king. The application of the knowledge Esther had gained about the Persian kingdom culture gave her power to act on behalf of the Jews.

+ Righteousness—refers to right conduct and behavior. Esther's motivation was righteousness when she spoke boldly before the king. The righteous are confident and bold as lions (Prov. 28:1).

+ Circumspection—means to carefully consider all related circumstances before acting, judging, or deciding; cautious; examining all the circumstances that may affect determination. Waiting gave Esther time to gather the facts (Esther 4:5).

+ Excellence—to be superior, to excel in anything.

+ Truth—the real facts about something; the reality and not falsehood.

+ Discretion—careful about what one says or does; thoughtfulness. Esther used discretion when she prepared a special dinner for King Ahasuerus

and Haman to assess the king's frame of mind
(Esther 5:5).

+ Fear of the Lord—Proverbs 9:10 says, "The fear of
the Lord is the beginning of wisdom." Wisdom
flows from a reverential awe of God and a deep
respect for God's ways. Esther was challenged by
her cousin Mordecai to overcome fear and indifference to save her people. It was her fear of the Lord
that caused her to move to action. Her respect
and awe for God outweighed her human fears.

+ Justice—giving to everyone what is due. It is
retributive. Esther by wisdom rewrote the decrees
that administered justice to Haman and his sons
and empowered the Jews to defend themselves.

Prayer and Fasting Release God's Justice

Of the increase of His government and peace there
will be no end, upon the throne of David and over His
kingdom, to order it and establish it with judgment
and justice from that time forward, even forever. The
zeal of the Lord of hosts will perform this.

—Isaiah 9:7

God is expanding and increasing the rule of His kingdom.
Therefore, He has to establish order and justice. This happens through His judgment and your prayers. Like Esther,
you have been strategically positioned as His queen over a
territory, and as you pray, you are establishing God's order
to things that have been out of order. Through prayer you
are operating under your mandate to bring kingdom order
to your sphere of influence—back into the earth realm. In

Isaiah 9:7 God is saying that the capacity, the size, and the influence of His government will be without end. As a queen in the kingdom, you rule and reign with Him through the scepter of prayer.

Jesus taught that justice would be established through night-and-day prayer (speaking God's Word). Justice is God making wrong things right. Jesus is the ultimate social reformer. He was the first to connect justice (social reform and making wrong things right) to night-and-day prayer. "Shall God not avenge [bring about justice for (NAS)] His own elect who cry out day and night to Him, though He bears long with them? I tell you that He will avenge [bring about justice to (NAS)] them speedily" (Luke 18:7–8).

Intercession positions us to hear from God and obey Him that we might walk in our callings and destinies. In intercession we position ourselves to receive revelation from His heart for our lives. In intercession we receive revelation into the destiny of people (loved ones), cities, or nations so that we may stand with them in contending for God's fullness for them.

Intercession for others causes multiplied blessings to return back on the life of the intercessor. Every prayer of blessing for another is a prayer that God returns back on you and your family. The law of the kingdom requires that we always receive more than what we give away by faith. "Give, and it will be given to you: good measure, pressed down, shaken together, and running over will be put into your bosom. For with the same measure that you use, it will be measured back to you" (Luke 6:38).

The International House of Prayer is known for their

intercession. In a teaching on the "Revelation of Intercession," it was said:

> Intercession is God's brilliant strategy for including the saints in ruling with Him in power. Yet it has such great impact on us as it draws us into intimacy with God as it protects with humility, transforms with holiness, anoints with power, unifies in community, releases revelation, and increases our inheritance while it trains us to rule with His wisdom.[1]

When you operate as a queen, you are in a position to partner with the King of kings to administrate justice. I have called this level of intercession kingly or governmental intercession because we are now sitting in high places, ruling and reigning with our brother Jesus Christ. We are no longer in a low position where we have to ask or petition. Because of Christ, believers are now seated as kings and queens commanding and decreeing, binding and loosing, allowing and disallowing—all through our prayers.

Prayer is the key to administrating the kingdom of God on the earth. That is why you may find that you face all kinds of opposition when you decide to go on a fast. All of hell hears your declaration. There is an invisible force that comes against you. Can you imagine what Esther faced? That's probably why she didn't fast alone. In the next chapter I will share with you what I believe Esther came up against during her fast. I believe these are things we have to face and defeat as modern-day Esthers before we are ready to move in our authority as queens.

PRAYER and FASTING MOVE US
INTO a NEW REALM of AUTHORITY

> Where the word of a king is, there is power; and who
> may say to him, "What are you doing?"
> —ECCLESIASTES 8:4

As I have said, the way we administrate the kingdom is by our words. Worlds are framed, wars are fought, and relationships are built or broken down by words, which form our prayers, which form our spirit of intercession. We must watch our words. We can't say that our families or our cities are going to hell in a handbasket because there are angels and demons watching over our words, waiting to perform the action you speak out.

There is an eternal glory that is rooted in intercession—governmental and kingly intercession. We will begin to activate the kingdom and move in the dimension of the kingdom through intercession. We can try and skip to all the decreeing and declaring, but if we don't first learn how to pray accurately, we will not transition to our place of authority. The Lord says that this is the hour when we really need to stand up and be the queens He designed us to be.

The war is not won until you get yourself into a place of prayer. Things will not shift in your life, your family life, your workplace, your city, state, or country until you pray. Esther knew this well.

When you get on your knees or position yourself at your church's night or morning prayer meetings, you are setting yourself in a place of authority to administrate and legislate the kingdom of God. Prayer is the scepter God designed for His queens and kings to extend as they rule and reign.

Through the scepter of prayer we will see His plans and purposes established in our lives and in the earth.

The Bible says that whatever we bind or permit will be bound or permitted in the earth (Matt. 16:19; 18:18). We can begin to speak a thing and it will be established (Job 22:28). We have the power through our prayers to stand as a gatekeeper and as a force against the powers of darkness. We have the power and authority to drive the devil out of the affairs of mankind. All the authority of the devil in the earthly realm is illegal. He doesn't have any delegated authority. The way he gets his power is through the actions of man. He operates through our choices. This is why fasting and prayer are so important. Our choices must become fully influenced by the power of the Holy Spirit.

There is a very real battle going on out there. The devil is taking no prisoners; he is out for blood; nations are raging. It was true in Esther's day, and it is true today.

Woman of God, you must stand in your jurisdiction. If you don't know what that is, ask God. He will tell you the territory He has given you. Our influence is not meant to be infinite and reach everywhere. It is important to know that God has not given us everything. A territory is "the extent or compass of a land within the bounds or belonging to the jurisdiction of any city, state, or other body."[2] Paul said, "I am not an apostle to everyone. I am not an apostle to the Jews. I am an apostle to the Gentiles." (See 1 Corinthians 9:2.) Some of us have not or will not see the effectiveness of our prayers and influence because we are out of territory. Every queen has a kingdom.

How do you get to understand your territory? You must stand in the counsel of the Lord.

PRAYER and FASTING USHER US
INTO the COUNSEL of the LORD

> For who has stood in the counsel of the LORD, and has perceived and heard His word? Who has marked His word and heard it?..."I have not sent these prophets, yet they ran. I have not spoken to them, yet they prophesied. But if they had stood in My counsel, and had caused My people to hear My words, then they would have turned them from their evil way and from the evil of their doings."
>
> —JEREMIAH 23:18–22

Women of God, we must be able to hear what God is saying to us about our territories—our families, our cities, our nations, and our workplaces. We cannot rely on what someone else says He says about them. In this season more than ever it is crucial for us to have the heavenly pattern for our lives. In order to see revival in these areas, we must stand in the counsel of the Lord.

The problem with the prophets in the above passage in Jeremiah is that they did not hear directly from God before they started speaking over God's people. Their words did not save those people from evil. But Esther's words did, and your words can too.

One of the keys to our queenly intercession is discernment, being able to know what God is saying. God has a specific word for the territories He has put us in authority over. Esther is our example. When she became awakened to her purpose, she immediately called a fast and went into three days of prayer. Esther knew that she could not be effective without going into the counsel of the Lord to seek His strategy for delivering His chosen people. He helped her discern His clear and accurate word for her territory, and He gave her the strategy for empowering her people and ultimately delivering them. What would have worked for the Jews in Jerusalem may not have worked so well for the Jews in Persia. Esther was strategically set in Persia to legislate God's justice on behalf of the nation of Israel. And she received that specific word from the Lord for that territory, and she moved to action.

We have to be careful to follow this pattern as well. Too much is at stake. There are lives attached to our being able to hear and discern what the Lord is saying. According to Matthew 16:18 our mandate is to bring and exercise the kingdom of God. But if we have not stood in the counsel of the King of kings and heard what He wants declared over a region, then we are not going to be in line with His kingdom mandates.

We need to have informed intercession. We can't just decree anything. Get in the counsel of the Lord. Let Him put His words in your mouth. Let Him download His truths to you. Prayer is a disciplined decision. First Peter 4:7 says, "But the end of all things is at hand; therefore be serious and watchful in your prayers." Prayer and intercession take us into the counsel of the Lord.

PRAYER and FASTING BREAK
HINDRANCES to the ESTHER ANOINTING

> Is this not the fast that I have chosen: to loose the
> bonds of wickedness, to undo the heavy burdens, to let
> the oppressed go free, and that you break every yoke?
> —ISAIAH 58:6

I am going to talk about this in much more detail in the
next chapter, but I wanted to touch on it here. Based on all
that Esther had gone through—being an orphan, being a
Jew in Persia, and even being a woman in a male-dominated
culture—I believe she had to overcome many spiritual obstacles and personal strongholds to get to a place where she
could walk in her authority as queen and bring deliverance
to her people. I believe that like many of us, she had to come
face-to-face with fear, shame, inadequacy, rejection, and even
a spirit of self-perseveration that gained entrance into her
life through what I call the orphan spirit. I believe that the
orphan spirit is one of the greatest hindrances to the Esther
anointing that must be broken through fasting and prayer.

Fasting releases the breaker anointing. In Isaiah 58 the
Lord talks to the prophet Isaiah about His chosen fast. This
is the fast the Lord says loosens the bonds of wickedness,
releases heavy burdens, frees the oppressed, and breaks every
yoke in our lives.

Women take on much of the burdens of our relationships. We hold in hurts and offenses. We work through and
persevere through enormous difficulties and injustices. But
through this we are open to demonic influences of all kinds.
Fasting will break these influences in our lives and cause us
to be confident and sure in God.

Fasting will also purify and transform our minds and our thinking. Fasting breaks the influence of our culture and aligns us with the culture of the kingdom. Fasting breaks limitations off our minds and causes us to expect to see the salvation of the Lord no matter the issue we are facing. Fasting purifies us and causes us to walk holy before the Lord, and it is our holiness and righteousness that will save us, our families, and our nations in the end.

Fasting also will release to us the characteristics I have identified as the Esther anointing. We will be empowered to make wise decisions and not react in our emotions. The wrong emotional perception could lead to wrong decisions. For example, if we believe and say to ourselves, "I can't start a new ministry because men will reject me," we will continue to make decisions that keep us from walking in the fullness God has for us. Our perceptions and mind-sets are largely based on tradition. This limits us. We choose according to how we perceive things. Fasting will set us free from that.

The grace of creative thinking, discerning of spirits, and strategic planning to deliver nations will be demonstrated in miraculous ways. Many of us are dealt the same amount of choices and possibilities like the great achievers we read about in history.

The only obstacle to our success is our choices in reactions to situations, how we express our love to others, how much hard work we are willing to put forth for our own success, and the words we chose to express ourselves—every little choice we make daily shapes our life. Fasting will break mental and spiritual strongholds that control us and set us free to live out our full purpose.

PRAYERS THAT RELEASE JUSTICE for WOMEN

Then your light shall break forth like the morning,
your healing shall spring forth speedily, and your righteousness shall go before you; the glory of the LORD
shall be your rear guard. Then you shall call, and the
LORD will answer.... The LORD will guide you continually, and satisfy your soul in drought, and strengthen
your bones.

—ISAIAH 58:8–11

*God, Your Word promises to break in with power to
those who embrace God's chosen fast (Isa. 58:6–12).
Father, I pray that You will demonstrate Your power
and justice for women worldwide. Let the light of
Your power break forth like the morning. Let healing and deliverance be ignited to bring an end to
the oppression of women and girls. Lord, righteousness and justice are the foundations of Your throne;
let righteousness be extended to women. Lord, raise
up deliverers who will execute justice that will help
relieve women from the bondage that results from
oppressive laws and social barriers that have been
created over decades or centuries. Lord, let modern-
day Esthers be set in governmental positions that will
give women a voice in the decision-making process.
Let women all over the world be empowered to break
the bonds of wickedness and heavy burdens. Let
every yoke be destroyed.*

*Lord, give me creative ideas on how to help the
oppressed. I will dream big and think outside the
box. I believe change is possible, and I want to be a*

> *part of the solution. Lord, give me creative ways to*
> *raise awareness of women's issues.*

The prophet Micah gave one of the best summaries of the kingdom lifestyle. We are called to be workers of justice and lovers of mercy with a spirit of humility (Micah 6:8). Works of justice include feeding the poor; caring for the needy, orphans, widows, and homeless; and helping to alleviate the oppression of abortion, poverty, misogyny, and racism (systemized prejudice) in the marketplace, law enforcement, education, employment, and so on. This is what God wants from us. This is how God wants us to live and what He will require from us.

Prayers for the prevention and abolishment of sex trafficking

Our prevention work begins and ends with Jesus Christ. Jesus has come to set the captives free (Luke 4:18). Sex trafficking thrives when it is hidden in the shadows. It becomes a well-kept secret—an out-of-sight, out-of-mind tragedy with victims who are unable to speak for themselves.

> *Lord, I pray for the end of human trafficking in*
> *all parts of the world. Lord, I pray that the light of*
> *Your glory will expose everything done in darkness.*
> *Let the issue of sex trafficking be brought to the fore-*
> *front of our nation. Raise up voices for the voiceless*
> *victims. Let the public become educated about the*
> *issue. I pray for the righteous organizations who seek*
> *to bring an end to this social tragedy that they will*
> *have all of the resources to create social awareness*

and give ways to eradicate sex trafficking around the world. In Jesus's name I pray. Amen.

More prayer targets for women's justice

+ Girls' education
+ Women and children's health
+ Economic empowerment
+ Domestic violence

Chapter 6

BREAK FREE FROM *the*
ORPHAN SPIRIT

[Mordecai] also gave him a copy of the decree to destroy them, that was given out in Shushan, that he might show it to Esther, explain it to her, and charge her to go to the king, make supplication to him, and plead with him for the lives of her people. And Hathach came and told Esther the words of Mordecai.

Then Esther spoke to Hathach and gave him a message for Mordecai, saying, All the king's servants and the people of the king's provinces know that any person, be it man or woman, who shall go into the inner court to the king without being called shall be put to death; there is but one law for him, except [him] to whom the king shall hold out the golden scepter, that he may live. But I have not been called to come to the king for these thirty days. And they told Mordecai what Esther said.

Then Mordecai told them to return this answer to Esther, Do not flatter yourself that you shall escape in the king's palace any more than all the other Jews. For if you keep silent at this time, relief and deliverance shall arise for the Jews from elsewhere, but you and your father's house

will perish. And who knows but that you have come to the
kingdom for such a time as this and for this very occasion.

Then Esther told them to give this answer to Mordecai,
Go, gather together all the Jews that are present in Shushan,
and fast for me; and neither eat nor drink for three days,
night or day. I also and my maids will fast as you do. Then
I will go to the king, though it is against the law; and if I
perish, I perish.

—ESTHER 4:8–16, AMP

WHEN PLACED IN disastrous situations it is amazing how
women can display great feats of strength. Eleanor Roosevelt states it best: "A woman is like a tea bag—you don't
know how strong she is until you put her in hot water."[1] It
is also in threatening times we have a tendency to hide and
draw back in fear. It is through traumatic ordeals that our
character is tested and we are forced to tap into hidden gifts,
wisdom, and ingenuity. It is through the storms of life that
character flaws are uncovered and refined, our true identities
are revealed, and we are transformed into the heroic, influential women God created us to be. The Lord causes the fire
of adversity to cause the dross in the heart to be purged, and
the heart is purified. He is committed to removing anything
that will hinder the fulfillment of His purposes in our lives.

I would like to use this chapter to uncover what I believe
is the greatest hindrance to the Esther anointing and per-
haps the greatest curse on the earth today—the orphan
spirit. Esther's reluctance and then sudden compliance to

her cousin Mordecai's demands to approach the king unannounced upon threat of death stem from a deeply rooted emotional battle with the orphan spirit.

In the beginning of the story of Queen Esther the author identifies Esther as being raised by her cousin Mordecai. Esther 2:7 states that Esther had neither father nor mother. In other words, she was an orphan. An orphan is a person who has been deprived by death of one or usually both parents. Someone who is fatherless has no identity as a son or daughter. Esther had a true identity crisis. She had been raised as a Jew but was forced to live as a Persian. The name Esther itself is an indication as to how she led her life and fulfilled her role. The root of Esther in Hebrew is *hester*, meaning "hidden." Some scholars believe Esther's name means hidden, reflecting her hidden identity. She had to hide her true identity. But I believe she was also hiding her inner struggle with the orphan spirit. It takes the eyes of discernment to see this spirit in many of Esther's responses and actions. It was the orphan spirit that caused Esther to respond to Mordecai with indifference and insecurity. The orphan spirit caused her to have fear about her position with her husband. Her initial response was rooted in self-preservation. Self-preservation is the fruit of an orphan spirit. It is in difficult times that we dig deep within to overcome our greatest obstacle to fulfilling destiny, which is "self." Esther overcomes herself and finds the courage to reveal her identity as a Jew regardless of the consequences.

I believe Mordecai used his words of authority to break through the strongman in Esther's life. I believe Esther's greatest obstacle was self-preservation rooted in the orphan spirit.

As I prepared to write this book, I often wondered why Mordecai's words to Esther were so strong. They seemed to be laced in a threat of death. Actually he really gave her no options but to face the king. Mordecai directly remarked that even if the queen should decide to continue to hide her Jewish identity, as he himself had previously advised, she would face certain death, but the Jews would be delivered by another source. Mordecai knew that Esther had a survivalist mentality. She had a tendency to protect herself and do whatever it took to survive. I am not vilifying Mordecai or Esther here. His words awakened her to both her need to overcome herself and embrace the possibility of a greater purpose.

Esther was a young woman placed in circumstances out of her control. We have all been there. Either take the risk and step out of the boat or sink. If Esther's statement, "I will go to the king, though it is against the law; and if perish, I perish" came from the mouth of a twenty-first-century woman, it would be, "I'm going to do what I have to do to survive."

Many times women are placed in situations where it seems as if there is no other alternative but to comply with the circumstance even if it means we lose our dignity and self-respect in the process. The Talmud clarifies that Esther's relationship with Ahasuerus wasn't a romantic one. It goes on to reveal that Esther remained passive the first night with the king and allowed him to rape her repeatedly. She performed and complied to survive. According to the Talmud

Esther had a difficult time her first six years in the palace. She remained passive to the king and obedient to her cousin Mordecai.[2] Her passivity and indifference to the plight of her people all stemmed from her lack of identity. This too was a fruit of the orphan spirit.

CHARACTERISTICS and SIGNS of the ORPHAN SPIRIT

The orphan spirit entered the planet at the fall of Adam and Eve. God was the center of man's world, and He provided for man and protected everything that He created. The major result of the fall is that man became the center of his own world. He orphaned himself and became alienated from God. When you become the center of your own universe, you become your own resource and you become afraid of God. A person with an orphan spirit is one who lacks emotional identity and seeks to earn her identity through her own efforts. What is a spiritual orphan? A spiritual orphan is one who feels alone; one who feels that she does not have a safe and secure place in the Father's heart where He can affirm, protect, provide, and express His love. She does not feel she belongs. She is full of fear, anxiety, and insecurity. Spiritual orphans have an independent spirit that often causes them to hide or deny pain.

The orphan spirit is always concerned with provision and protection. This worry causes them to operate in their own abilities apart from God. The orphan spirit moves out of self-sufficiency, creating fig leaves to protect oneself from being seen by the Creator. Going back to the story of Adam and Eve, we see this same action. It is one of shame and an attempt to cover or hide one's wrongs or weaknesses. (See Genesis 3:7.)

A person who operates out of an orphan spirit constantly harbors feelings of abandonment, loneliness, alienation, and isolation. Esther was isolated and alienated from her family and forced to live in a pagan world. Her peace and security were taken, and she was forced to comply in order to survive. Those who operate out of an orphan heart never want to rebel against those in authority for this may jeopardize their security.

1. The orphan spirit operates out of insecurity and fear. When Esther was not summoned for thirty days, she did not know if the king had found someone more pleasing or if she was merely losing her influence. Even though Scripture states that the King loved Esther more than all the women in the entire kingdom, she was not secure in his love. Many times orphans have an inability to receive love.

2. The orphan spirit causes you to be performance oriented. Esther won favor with the king. "When the turn came for Esther (the young woman Mordecai had adopted, the daughter of his uncle Abihail) to go to the king, she asked for nothing other than what Hegai, the king's eunuch who was in charge of the harem, suggested. And Esther won the favor of everyone who saw her" (Esther 2:15, NIV). When we take a look at this scripture in the New International Version, it says Esther

"won favor," indicating that favor wasn't just given or bestowed upon her but it indicates something that she was doing. I believe Esther was gracious and well mannered, but her heart was one that believed, "I have to perform or give it everything I have to become number one."

3. The orphan spirit causes you to always be in an inner competition with others. This spirit dictates that you must stand out at all cost. The orphan spirit gains its identity from being better than everyone else.

4. The orphan spirit lacks self-esteem and identity.

5. The orphan spirit is self-reliant. When family life is dramatically disrupted, the orphan will only depend on what they can control. Esther was suddenly taken from her family life. She may have felt that she had no one else to lean upon but herself.

6. The orphan spirit is self-protecting. Orphans feel unsure about their position. They feel uncovered and unprotected; therefore the instinct is to protect themselves.

7. The orphan spirit is deeply rooted in self-preservation. Self-preservation occurs when you obsess on protecting the things you are afraid of losing. Mordecai challenged Esther's fear of losing everything she had worked so hard to gain. We must understand when we become obsessed with protecting the very things we are afraid of losing, we

tend to lose them more quickly. Mark 8:34–35 says, "Then he called the crowd to him along with his disciples and said: 'Whoever wants to be my disciple must deny themselves and take up their cross and follow me. For whoever wants to save their life will lose it, but whoever loses their life for me and for the gospel will save it'" (NIV).

DELIVERANCE FROM the ORPHAN SPIRIT

It's only after fasting and praying that Esther seems confident and takes on a leadership role in the story. After fasting, prayer, and being delivered from an orphan spirit, Esther, "initially a beautiful young woman with a weak character…becomes transformed into a person with heroic moral stature and political skill."[3]

I believe in the time of fasting and prayer the Lord delivered her from the bondage of an orphan spirit. This is how we can explain Esther's abrupt change in behavior from deep despair to determined action and from passiveness to leadership. During her time of fasting, Esther connected with her inner self and understood why she had been made queen. She understood why she had to suffer through her relationship with this irritable king. She found confidence in the presence of the Lord. She understood that she had a mission and that she could shape reality rather than passively suffer through it. Esther had been made queen to save her people; her mission and her faith shaped her character and inspired her to act and succeed.

Throughout our lives we all face crisis from time to time. Sometimes the crises are severe, threatening the stability and security of our lives. It is in this time our true identities are tested and perfected. We must embrace the Father's love and acceptance. Women are not second-class citizens in the kingdom; we are Daddy's girls. He has already declared the end from the beginning; His plans for us are good and not evil. We must be healed from father rejection. We are not orphans, we have received the spirit of adoption, and we can cry out to Him, Abba, Father. God the Father's love protects and sustains.

PRAYER THAT BREAKS the ORPHAN SPIRIT

Lord, I thank You that You love me. I receive Your love. Let the power of Your blood cleanse me from an orphan spirit. Baptize my heart with the fire of Your love. Let the fire of Your love burn away the rejection and fear. Let the fire of Your love purge away the dross of the orphan spirit. Your love is like vehement flames, and many waters cannot quench Your love for me. The flames of Your love for me are eternal, and many floods will never be able to drown it out. Your Word says that You will not leave us as orphans but You will come to us.

Holy Spirit, come and pour the love of God in my heart. Holy Spirit, teach me how to receive the love of the Father. Come empower me with the truth of Your love. I loose myself from the survivalist mentality. I don't want to just survive; I want to enjoy the abundant life You have for me. I am tired of making fig leaves for myself. I am tired of living in fear and shame. I will no longer hide from Your presence.

I humble myself, Lord. Your Word says that unless a kernel of wheat falls to the ground and dies, it will not bear fruit. I choose to die to self. I will not only be concerned with my best interest, but I will also use my authority to benefit the well-being of others. I shake myself free from passivity and indifference.

I am a daughter of the King. I am not an orphan. I don't have to perform to receive Your love. I receive the spirit of adoption, and I cry, "Abba, Father." I loose myself from all insecurity and fear. I loose myself from self-preservation.

Forgive me for being obsessed with trying to keep things I've obtained through striving and competing. No longer will I compete to survive. I have favor with You. I trust Your love to protect me. I find my security in You. You are my heavenly Father; You provide for me. I choose to obey Your Word. I will no longer try to save my life but lose it in the arms of Your love. Amen.

Chapter 7

WALK *in* BOLDNESS *and* COURAGE

When I called, you answered me; you greatly emboldened me.
—PSALM 138:3, NIV

IN FACING ANY desperate situation, there is a need for courage. How could we as modern-day women imagine the fear and insecurity that would plague Queen Esther, who was chosen solely on the basis of her beauty and appeal to the king? Esther had to search within herself to embrace courage and boldness against unbelievable odds with relentless determination to persevere.

She didn't have the Bible or a pastor she could seek for counsel. She was no princess with the clout of her father's kingdom to enhance her position in the court. When she was not summoned for thirty days (Esther 4:11), she did not know if the king had found someone more pleasing or if she was merely losing her influence. She had the struggle that we all have in this pagan society that is adverse to the kingdom of God: How do we respond boldly, wisely, and faithfully to difficult circumstances that come our way and over which we sometimes seem to have little or no control?

This inner struggle with fear of death is something every

great leader faces. I don't mean death in the physical sense but death to our reputation, death to the pride of life, death to the opinions of men, and even death to success. We must step out of our comfort zones, let go of the events and misfortunes that try to haunt and hinder our success. We must step out of the boat of fear and timidity and walk on the water with courage and boldness.

After fasting and prayer, there must be a corresponding action. Esther uses her life as an instrument of intercession. She had to do something. As a displaced, orphaned Jewess, Esther had been reared by Mordecai, her older relative. She knew Jewish laws and custom. She had worshiped Yahweh. Could she trust in His delivering hand although the situation looked hopeless? She had already overcome many obstacles, endured the beautification process, and now she had found some sense of peace and security. This was definitely not the time to rock the boat.

I would like to say that timing is always the excuse the enemy will use to stop women from fulfilling the call of God on our lives. We argue that we have to raise the children. Some of us say, "I will follow the call of God when my kids are grown and off to college," "I have to support my husband," "take care of my mother," and the list goes on and on. While all of these are important tasks, we must not let them become an obstacle to boldly and courageously obeying the call of God on our lives. God has perfect timing for everything He does. Creation was established upon the perfect timing of the omniscient Creator. He holds our times in His hands.

Faced with a desperate challenge to survival, Esther

pondered Mordecai's question: "Who knows whether you have come to the kingdom for such a time as this?" I believe Mordecai was alluding to the call of God on Esther's life. Mordecai points out that all of the previous circumstances of Esther's life that led her to the Persian throne may have been just for this moment when she can intercede for her people. I believe his words challenged and reminded Esther that a place of privilege can never exempt a person from responsibility to respond to God's call.

Do you feel that there is something calling you to a rewarding and fulfilling life? We are all called by God to accomplish His purpose in the earth. So many of us miss out on the call of God for our lives because we are not awake or aware of the simple ways God wants to involve us in His plan.

Many traditional churches have not trained women to lead, but I believe all of this is changing. Many women are being liberated in their minds and belief systems from conservative, traditional churches that have held them in bondage and oppression. Like Esther, we must assume the dignity and power of our royal positions and boldly and courageously claim our true identities as women called of God. Women are being empowered to bring healing and deliverance to society. There is a deficit of bold Christian women among the ranks of leaders in the land. We must embrace the call of God to be His change agents in the earth.

The CALL to ACTIVE DUTY

There is a set time for a move of God in every generation, and within His church. There are some things that are the express will of God, and they will not change or move because they are in alignment with God's purpose. God is giving a clarion call for women to rise up and proclaim His Word throughout the land. God is awakening an army of women to His eternal purposes in the earth. He is equipping them with a spirit of boldness to face cultural threats against women worldwide.

We will not keep silent. We will speak out against injustice and oppression. We must respond appropriately to the call of God. There is an established timing for the process of God's call, assignment, dream, or purpose in your life to be discovered, walked, and fulfilled. I want to proclaim to you: Woman of God, this is your set time.

There are several things we must learn about the call of God. The call of God for your life began in the heart of God. Jeremiah 1:5 says, "I knew you before I formed you in your mother's womb. Before you were born I set you apart and appointed you" (NLT). The call of God is eternal. We are called to glorify God with our lives. Our calling is God's idea, and it is His purpose for our lives. The call of God for our lives originated in eternity, and it proceeded from His heart not from our wills or imaginations, or from anyone else's will or imagination.

There is a process to discovering the call of God on your life. Now that you are awakened to the call, you must be prepared by the Holy Spirit. This involves personal interaction with the Spirit of God and an understanding of what God is speaking to you.

The Process of God's Call

I have seen the painful labor and exertion and miserable business which God has given to the sons of men with which to exercise and busy themselves. He has made everything beautiful in its time. He also has planted eternity in men's hearts and minds [*a divinely implanted sense of a purpose working through the ages which nothing under the sun but God alone can satisfy*], yet so that men cannot find out what God has done from the beginning to the end.

—Ecclesiastes 3:10–11, amp,
emphasis added

1. The ignorance stage (Acts 9:4–19)

In this initial stage of development, God gives you a calling, assignment, dream, or promise, and you have no understanding of what it is or how it is supposed to function. You are wondering why God chose you for this calling, and you are looking around at the ability of others, wondering why God did not call them instead of you. Everyone else seems to be better qualified and better equipped.

At the same time you are also wondering why you feel so compelled toward a particular area of ministry or service. This dilemma stirs a desire to seek God about the call on your life. Like Paul in Acts 9, you begin to ask questions of the Lord and of yourself:

+ "Who are You, Lord?" (v. 5). The answer to this question also reveals who you are. You are made in His image, and the more you get to know the character of God, the more you will know the way He has designed you to reflect Him in the earth.

"What do You want me to do?" (v. 6) The answer to this question is the opening of clarification and direction for His call on your life. Now, ask yourself:

+ Who is Jesus to me?

+ Who am I to Jesus?

+ What does Jesus want me to do in His kingdom?

2. The full-depth stage (Phil. 3:10–14)

In this stage you desire to discover the full depth of your calling, assignment, or dream. In order to know your calling, you must first know the One who did the calling. Knowing the God of the dream opens clarity and understanding about the call on your life.

Ask yourself:

+ In what ways have I been stagnant or neutral about pursuing the purpose of God for my life?

+ What is required of me to change this position of stagnation and neutrality?

3. The comprehension stage (2 Tim. 1:11–12)

In this stage you come to know and understand some of the depths, requirements, and specifics of your call. The initial fear and anxiety has calmed down, and you have become confident in accepting the call of God. "For I know whom I have believed, and am persuaded" (v. 12).

Paul moved from not knowing God, to wanting to know God, and then his desire was fulfilled as he began to relate with the God of the call. You will know God in increasing levels of relational intimacy through worship, prayer, and the Word. You will become confident of what God has called you to do—His purpose. You will be persuaded that the God of the call is able to make sure that His calling is fulfilled in your life.

Ask yourself:

+ How am I growing in my relationship with Jesus?
+ How would I describe my level of confidence in my assignment?

4. The fulfillment stage (2 Tim. 4:6–8; Acts 26:12–19)

In this stage you are living with the assurance that the instructions assigned to you in the call of God have been fulfilled or carved out to their fullest expression. This assurance produces a desire for a reward. You realize that there is a reward for those who complete God's assignment according to His blueprint for their lives.

You will realize that you have fought a good or honorable fight.

You will realize that you have finished your course or your assignment.

You will also realize that you have kept the faith, or remained in courage and trust in God and His ability to fulfill everything He has declared for your life.

You will submit yourself to the price or sacrificial demands of God's call, and from that posture of humility you will evoke a response from God, receiving your reward.

> But without faith it is impossible to please and be satisfactory to Him. For whoever would come near to God must [necessarily] believe that God exists and

that He is the rewarder of those who earnestly and
diligently seek Him [out].

—HEBREWS 11:6, AMP

At this stage it is important that you believe that God is
actively engaged in every detail of your life and that He will
reward you if you are continually pursuing Him.

DEFINING BIBLICAL BOLDNESS and COURAGE

As I stated at the beginning of this chapter, we need boldness and courage to walk in God's call on our lives or else we
will give into all the traps, discouragement, and distractions
from the enemy. Let's take a closer look at both of the bib-
lical attributes and see how they propel us into our call.

Bold as a lioness

In Acts 4:29–31 *boldness* is the Greek word *parrhesia*. It
is characterized by "outspokenness, unreserved utterance,
freedom of speech, with frankness, candor, cheerful courage,
and the opposite of cowardice, timidity, or fear."[1] In this
verse "it denotes a divine enablement that comes to ordinary
and unprofessional people exhibiting spiritual power and
authority. It also refers to a clear presentation of the gospel
without being ambiguous or unintelligible. *Parrhesia* is not
a human quality but a result of being filled with the Holy
Spirit."[2]

Boldness is confidence in Him. When you are made perfect in love—because perfect love casts out all fear—you can
be bold because you know God. God is love. You can't love
without God, and you can't be bold without God.

This is a pivotal part of the Esther anointing. Esther

would not have had the boldness to speak to the king about her people if she had not prayed and fasted, been filled with the heart of God for her people, and then been emboldened with righteous indignation to risk death to see them through to their deliverance. You will not get this anointing without praying.

Some of us won't step out or take action toward the call of God because we are full of fear. We are like the Cowardly Lion from *The Wizard of Oz*. We are afraid of losing our reputations and being rejected. When I look over in Revelation, do you know that the cowardly and the unbelieving are all in that lake of fire?

> But the cowardly, unbelieving, abominable, murderers, sexually immoral, sorcerers, idolaters, and all liars shall have their part in the lake which burns with fire and brimstone, which is the second death.
>
> —REVELATION 21:8

Woman of God, that is not God's ordained future for you. The Word says that "the righteous are bold as a lion" (Prov. 28:1). There is a roar that is going to come out of Zion, and it is going to come from that "great company of women who will boldly bring the good news to the earth through their gifts, talents, wisdom, and creativity. (See Psalm 68:11, HCSB.)

As mentioned before, boldness is a divine enablement that comes upon ordinary and unprofessional people causing them to exhibit spiritual power and authority. A supernatural boldness causes you to confront the things that come against Jesus and His name. If we were all honest here, we would admit that we are scared most of the time. That's OK. We can admit to the Lord that we are scared. We can ask Him for boldness just to open our mouths, and He will do the rest. It is by His Spirit that the hearts of people are influenced. He is the one who convicts mankind of sin. All we need to do is have the courage and boldness to open our mouths.

Courageous conviction

Courage is the strength of mind to carry on in spite of danger. Courage doesn't deny imminent danger; it denies danger's authority over your life. Courage and boldness are sometimes used interchangeably. Here is the compound meaning of courage:

+ Choosing to act in the face of danger; moral bravery that involves acting in a way that enhances what one believes; to be good in spite of social disapproval and possible backlash. In a nutshell it is standing for what is right in the midst of what could be a life-threatening situation.

+ Following the convictions your heart.

+ Persevering in the face of adversity. In order to persevere with a task, a person must be able to suppress desires to give up and pursue an easier task. For this person the purpose of God becomes preeminent.

+ Standing up for justice.

+ Facing suffering with dignity and faith.

+ Letting go of the familiar.

Courageously Esther formulated her plan, even if it meant dying in the effort. In the court she had been taught to pre-pare herself physically, but she had also learned to prepare herself spiritually, as was evidenced by her fasting (Esther 4:16; 9:31). Esther had to overcome her fears and rise to meet destiny. Her biggest obstacle to overcome was self-preservation. Self-preservation is the complete opposite of courage.

With courage, Esther seized the right moment, presented her case, not questioning the king's justice or righteousness, and humbly asked for mercy for herself and her people.

Divine guidance obviously directed Esther's thoughts, words, and actions. She had won the respect and the ear of her royal husband. In response he assigned to her the task of re-writing the law (see Esther 9:29), and she became quite properly the heroine of her people.

What Are You Afraid Of?

> Then said I: "Ah, Lord God! Behold, I cannot speak, for I am a youth." But the Lord said to me: "Do not say, 'I am a youth,' for you shall go to all to whom I send you, and whatever I command you, you shall speak. Do not be afraid of their faces, for I am with you to deliver you," says the Lord. Then the Lord put forth His hand and touched my mouth, and the Lord said to me: "Behold, I have put My words in your mouth. See, I have this day set you over the nations and over the kingdoms, to root out and to pull down, to destroy and to throw down, to build and to plant."
> —Jeremiah 1:6–10

Esther had some fears and excuses to contend with during her three-day fast. What are your excuses? What are your fears? For the prophet Jeremiah, he claimed that he was too young. But God came back and told him that He would be with him, that He would put His words in his mouth, and that He had established him. God has established you to walk as a queen in the kingdom of God, writing and rewriting decrees that cause His kingdom to expand. When you sit in the counsel of God, He will equip you with resources, favor, passion, and strategy. He will not leave you alone. He will fill you with His Spirit to carry out His call on your life. He has set you up and established you to rout out all the powers of the enemy in your territory.

Now let's rewrite the devil's decrees against our families, our cities, and our nations. He has no authority over the territories God has already promised to us. The enemy's word over our lives will not stand. With boldness and courage, we pull it down in the name of Jesus!

PRAYER to ACTIVATE
BOLDNESS and COURAGE

Now, Lord, look upon the threats of the enemy and grant to me the spirit of boldness that I may preach Your Word with miracles, signs, and wonders. Stretch Your mighty hand over my life; empower me with right words at the right time. My confidence and trust is in You. Lord, give me courage to confront in love those who oppose Your Word.

I decree that I am a fearless and bold woman of God. I will answer the call to be an instrument of change in the earth. I will respond in crisis. I will boldly proclaim the gospel. In moral crisis I will boldly stand for truth. I will not be muzzled by the laws of the land. I will open my mouth wide, and You will fill it.

God, give me Your heart for my assignment. Give me Your perspective that I might be Your mouthpiece in the earth. I will stand up against injustice. I am the righteousness of God, and I am bold like a lion. I am fearless in the face of danger. I will preach the Word. I will go wherever You send me. In Jesus's name I pray. Amen.

Chapter 8

REWRITE *the* DECREE

You yourselves write a decree concerning the Jews, as you
please, in the king's name, and seal it with the king's signet
ring; for whatever is written in the king's name and sealed
with the king's signet ring no one can revoke.

—ESTHER 8:8

My tongue is the pen of a ready writer.

—PSALM 45:1

A DECREE IS AN official order, edict, or decision. A decree is
something that seems to be foreordained. A decree can also
mean to order, decide officially, appoint a group or person to
accomplish something. It can ban, outlaw, or restrict. This
process is linked to binding and loosing. (See Matthew 18:18.)
It causes what is proclaimed or decreed to come into manifestation. A decree is forthtelling. It speaks for the counsel of
God. If you don't stand in the counsel of the Lord, how can
you make a decree? How can you release the heart and mind
of God for a given situation, people, or territory?

> You will make your prayer to Him, and He will hear
> you, and you will pay your vows. You shall also decide

and decree a thing, and it shall be established for you; and the light [of God's favor] shall shine upon your ways. When they make [you] low, you will say, [There is] a lifting up; and the humble person He lifts up and saves. He will even deliver the one [for whom you intercede] who is not innocent; yes, he will be delivered through the cleanness of your hands.

—Job 22:27–30, amp

You must be a woman of revelation. A spirit of revelation is a special endowment to perceive and look into the deep plans of God. God wants you to understand that, as you walk in the Esther anointing, you are no longer praying upward; you are praying downward. You have been seated with Jesus in high places. God wants you to understand your position in the spirit. Too long we have walked bowed down, defeated, and afraid. But you have now been emboldened with the love, grace, and humility of Christ, and He has elevated you to rule and reign with Him in the earth (Eph. 1:20; 2:6).

From this high position as a queen in the kingdom of God, you are praying downward. No longer are you just asking, but also you are writing and rewriting decrees. Through your prayers, you are administrating the kingdom of God in the earth. As we have already discovered, this level of intercession is different than other kinds of intercession. This is not worship. This is not prayers about meeting individual needs only. You are operating in a different realm. This is governmental level intercession—the kind that kings and queens in the kingdom operate by. At this level your prayers are decrees permitting things that are lawful and restricting things that are illegal.

The Power of Proclamations and Decrees

When a proclamation was released or announced, the town crier or herald would shout the news through the city streets. The decree was written and posted at the city gates and in the important town centers for all to see. The decree changed the normal course of life. It indicated that, regardless of what life was like before, a shift had taken place and things were commanded to change. Whatever the demand of the decree, it necessitated obedience and usually required a response from the people. It said: "Line up or face the consequences."[1]

In the kingdom of God, decrees are the proclamation of the will and Word of the Lord into the spirit realm. In Hebrew the word *decree* is *gazar*, which means "to cut down or cut off, to destroy, divide, exclude, or decide."[2] *Gazar* expresses the characteristics of a decree. It also describes the office of the prophet and the power behind the spoken mind of God.

In Job 22:28 (kjv) the word *thing* is the Hebrew word *omer*, which means "a word, speech, or a promise."[3] *Establish* is the Hebrew word *qum*, which means "not only to establish, but also to arise or stand."[4] Therefore this verse can be read as, "You shall decide a command and it will rise up, grow, and be established, rushing forth because of you."

Decrees issue sudden breakthrough in all manners of situations. Decrees are at the basis, the foundation, of breakthrough. They release the ability to do whatever is needed to break the power of Satan in any given situation. In this case, it is powerful praying and making decrees to the thing that needs to be broken.

The Eternal Decree

I want to show you something about the eternal decree. Let's
take a look at Psalm 2:7-9:

> I will declare the decree: the LORD has said to Me,
> "You are My Son, today I have begotten You. Ask of
> Me, and I will give You the nations for Your inheri-
> tance, and the ends of the earth for Your possession.
> You shall break them with a rod of iron; you shall
> dash them to pieces like a potter's vessel."

Here, God is saying, "I have done everything that I am
going to do. I have given you the authority to bind. I have
given you the authority to loose." See, it's not about just
getting up and coming out to a nice prayer meeting and
saying, "Present and accounted for." No! It's about walking
into your created dimension, walking in what God created
you to do.

Your words have power. Life or death comes by the words
you speak. You can begin to create in the heavens by your
words. So when you stand and say, "There shall be no terrorism in my city. I decree it by the power of God. I bind
every spirit of terrorism in the name of Jesus," it stops the
works of darkness. The words that we pray in this hour, the
things that we say, will affect the quality of life because God
has decreed the eternal decree that sets us as kings and
queens over the earth.

Coming together corporately as kings and queens on the
earth and praying is not just about a few breakthroughs. We
will begin to see our intercession as a governmental act that
releases decrees and edicts into the earthly realm. We will

begin to see our decrees take effect on what's going on in our cities and in our homes. God has set a company of women in the earth for such a time as this. We will begin to govern like the queens we are, writing and rewriting decrees and overthrowing the spirit of Haman that is rising against the kingdom.

What I want to do in this book is give you a broader scope of why you have been called to be a modern-day Esther, why you have been anointed, why the Lord has set His words in your mouth, and why the Lord has set your tongue as the pen of a ready writer. I want to charge and challenge you in your spirit. I want you to understand that your prayers will save your life and your children's lives. The prayers that you pray will deliver nations. God said too long we have erred in not knowing the authority that we have on the inside of us. For after all, the kingdom is on the inside of us, and we release it through our prayers.

This is the eternal decree of the Lord Jesus Christ, and it will not be returned to Him void. It doesn't matter how much the devil comes against you, the eternal decree has given you authority to say with a loud voice: "You will fall, devil. I don't care what you say. There is an ancient decree that's been decreed from eternity past. I will see the glory of God in my city. The kingdom of God will advance! So I will pray! I will stand watch. I will see the salvation of the Lord."

When we gather corporately, we're not just coming to pray nice little prayers. We're coming to create an atmosphere where the power of God can flow. We're coming to stop the plans of the enemy. How we rewrite the decrees of the enemy against God's people will affect the way we live and the generations to come. The wisest choice you can make is to join with a body of believers in corporate prayer and begin to govern in the heavens.

In the next chapter I am going to talk about how God is healing the relationships between women and men and moving us together in unity and respect to corporately increase the advancement of God's kingdom. But first let's rewrite some decrees!

DECREES TO PRESERVE MY FAMILY AND FUTURE GENERATIONS

I **decree** that the seed of the righteous shall be delivered from every evil plot against their destiny (Prov. 11:21).

I **decree** that my descendants will be mighty on the earth (Ps. 112:2).

I **decree** that the generation of the upright shall be blessed. Wealth and riches shall be in our house, and our righteousness shall endure forever (Ps. 112:3).

I **decree** that my children and my children's children will worship the name of the Lord Jesus Christ (Ps. 145:4).

I **break** all limitations set by the enemy against my descendants' lives. I decree that they shall live and not die and declare the works of the Lord (Ps. 118:17).

I **decree** that no weapon formed against my family line shall prosper (Isa. 54:17).

I **decree** increase, expansion, and enlargement in the earth (Ps. 115:14–16).

I **decree** that my children shall be taught of the Lord Jesus Christ (Isa. 54:13).

I **decree** God's everlasting mercy and peace shall rest upon my children (Isa. 54:13).

I **decree** that the goodness and mercy of the Lord shall follow my children all the days of their lives and my children shall dwell in the house of the Lord forever (Ps. 23:6).

I **decree** that my entire family shall be saved (Acts 16:31).

Decrees for My City

I **decree** peace within the streets of my city (Deut. 20:10).

I **decree** that every assignment of violence and murder in my city will be broken (Ps. 55:9).

I **decree** that the river of God is flowing in my city (Ps. 46:4).

I **decree** that the voice of the Lord is heard in my city (Ps. 29:3).

I **decree** that my city belongs to Jesus, the great King (Ps. 48:2).

I **decree** that the Lord defends my city (Isa. 37:35).

I **decree** that the businesses in my city flourish like the grass of the earth (Ps. 72:16).

I **decree** that the Lord is watching over my city (Ps. 127:1).

I **decree** that the righteous have favor in my city (Prov. 11:10).

I **decree** that the Lord shall not forsake my city (Isa. 62:12).

I **decree** that revival will break out in my city.

I **decree** that the power of God is released in my city.

I **decree** great joy is being released in my city (Acts 8:8).

I **decree** that a multitude of people will be saved in my city (Acts 18:10).

I **decree** that God is the builder and maker of my city (Heb. 11:10).

I **decree** that the spiritual name of my city is "THE LORD IS THERE" (Ezek. 48:35).

PRAYER for REVIVAL AMONG the NATIONS

Lord, I decree that my country, my nation, and my people belong to You. I ask, Father, for Your blessings on my nation. Let the beliefs and morals of your kingdom be established. Lord, I humble myself. I am praying, seeking Your face, turning from my wicked ways, and petitioning You to heal my land. I ask that You will come and rain down righteousness in the land. Let all wickedness and perversion be cleansed from my land. Lord, awaken human hearts to Your love. Let the power of conviction return to pulpits. Let the preachers preach the gospel of Your kingdom.

Let there be an increased awareness of Your presence, God, and a new hunger for righteousness. Father, I desire to see Your glory cover the earth like the waters cover the sea. Let Your manifested presence return to the earth.

Let revival break out in my country. Let the kingdom of God break in with power. Let miracles, signs, and wonders be released in my land. Let every manner of disease and sickness be healed. Let the fame of Jesus spread across this nation, from coast to coast. In Jesus's name I pray. Amen.

Chapter 9

TEAMWORK MAKES
the DREAM WORK

God created man in his own image, in the image of God
created he him; male and female created he them. And
God blessed them, and God said to them, Be fruitful, and
multiply, and replenish the earth and subdue it: and have
dominion over the fish of the sea, and over the fowl of the
air, and over every living thing that moveth upon the earth.

—Genesis 1:27–28

THERE ARE TWO things we need to know: 1) woman as well
as man was created in the image of God. God did not create
woman to be inferior to man; both are equally important;
and 2) the woman was also expected to have authority over
God's creation. Man and woman are to share this authority—
it does not belong only to the man.

God has a redemptive plan for women. *Redemption* means
to pay the fine for someone who has been in prison. The Lord
Jesus Christ redeemed women from the curse and restored to
us authority to rule with men. Jesus changed the status of
women. We are no longer to be placed at man's feet but at
his side. God said, "It is not good that the man should be

alone; I will make him a helper fit for him" (Gen. 2:18, RSV). So God "caused a deep sleep to fall upon Adam, and he slept: and He took one of his ribs" (Gen. 2:21). God used that rib in the creation of Eve. This account shows how important the woman is to a man: she is part of his very being, and without her man is incomplete.

Women and men must be renewed in the spirit of their minds. If true partnerships are going to be formed and developed between the genders, we must be healed and delivered from demonic dysfunctions. We must first acknowledge who the real enemy to unity has been—Satan. We must get new definitions regarding the roles of men and women leading together. There must be a letting down of the guards. We must learn how to trust the God in one another. We must make a decision to be healed, delivered, and reconciled to one another. We must forget those things that are behind and reach forward to the things ahead.

LOOSE YOURSELVES, DAUGHTERS OF ZION!

> Shake yourself from the dust; arise, sit [erect in a dignified place], O Jerusalem; loose yourself from the bonds of your neck, O captive Daughter of Zion.
>
> —ISAIAH 52:2, AMP

Satan has a plan to continue to oppress women. He wants to snare and entrap us with pains of the past. He wants to keep us in a vicious cycle of blaming and pointing the finger at men. This is the season to take responsibility for our healing and deliverance. We must reconcile within ourselves that we may never get an apology or an acknowledgement of the injustices against us.

Many times it's not justice that we want; it's vengeance. Justice seeks to make wrong things right. Vengeance wants to make someone suffer and pay for the damage done. We must not allow bitterness to defile our anointing and stifle our growth. The Lord will give us strategies to overcome inequality while sustaining a godly spirit.

It is time to forgive and loose ourselves from pains that happen in our lives and in the church. We must consciously remove barriers to unity and teamwork. Here is a list of entrapments that are hindrances women and men need to overcome to form healthy male-female teamwork.

The "because I'm a woman" entrapment

If women are going to work with men in team ministry, we must not see everything through the lens of rejection. We must not think that everything a man does is injustice because we're women. I can remember working with a team of men at a conference and everyone's video was placed on the website—except mine. The devil instantly begin to put thoughts in my mind saying, "They're doing that to you because you are a woman. No one else's video got left off of the site." I immediately shut him down with the truth. I had a great relationship with the host and knew his heart was to promote my ministry. I knew it was just an oversight or technical difficulties. We must rightly judge every situation and cast down every imagination that exalts itself against the knowledge of God.

The contempt for men entrapment

In our story the king and his advisors believed that Queen Vashti's refusal to submit to the king's authority would influence women all over the kingdom, causing them to act in contempt of their husbands and be disrespectful to them. (See Esther 1:17–18.) We must be careful that our use of authority is not perceived as contempt for men. Contempt can be defined as feeling that someone or something is not worthy of any respect or approval. It is also a lack of respect for or fear of something that is usually respected. As we move and operate in our gifts and callings, we must exercise wisdom and humility. There may be times when we don't agree with our male counterparts, but we must be sensitive to the leading of the Holy Spirit in how we handle these issues. Everything does not need to be confronted, yet there are times when our cooperating with a course of action is not in line with God's will. There must be a balance between confrontation and cooperation.

The "I won't be taken advantage of again" entrapment

The Lord is raising up men in the earth who will have the Father's heart toward women. Hegai the eunuch represents those men who will see the giftings and talents in women. Hegai saw Esther's potential not just her physical beauty. He didn't have a sexual desire toward her. His motives were pure. He gave her advice and resources, and positioned her to win favor with the king. He also represents those men in the world who have knowledge and wisdom to impart that will prepare us for the next level of ministry. He mentored Esther in the rules of the palace and explained the decree of death to her.

The "I'll use a woman because I can't find a man" entrapment

Men must be delivered from the erroneous teaching that when God can't find a man, He will use a woman. Many base this teaching from Judges 4:9, where Barak, a leader in the army of Israel, didn't want to go to war, so the prophetess Deborah said she would go with him. Contrary to popular teaching, I believe Barak is an example of a man of faith who acknowledged the skill, leadership, and wisdom of God to have a woman anointed by God on his team. He didn't agree with the popular opinion of the day. He understood the power of the team. He knew that their combined efforts would ensure the success of the army as each brought their distinct, God-given strengths to the battle. Barak is listed among the heroes of faith in Hebrews 11:32. Women and men must maintain a heart of humility. Our priority must be accomplishing the will of God and giving Him all of the glory.

ESTHER and MORDECAI: The DREAM TEAM

It is clear throughout the story of Esther that God sovereignly chose to use Mordecai and Esther in His plan to deliver His people. Here we see a team that was willing to take a risk. Mordecai, who mentored Esther, challenged her fears and awakened the courage inside of her to go before the king. His counsel gave her perspective.

I have found many times as a woman that I allow my emotions to cause me to lose perspective on the big picture when it relates to my call and destiny. It's usually the male mentors in my life who cause me to see the big picture. Your mentor will have more faith for you than you have for yourself. You may not be able to find the perfect mentor, but you should be able to find a person, or various people, who can impart to you the qualities and skills you need to accomplish your assignments.

I would like to give a word of caution as it relates to men mentoring women. I'm not implying that men and women should spend time alone in mentoring sessions. Mentoring is a relational experience through which one person empowers another by sharing God-given resources.

The primary mentor for a woman should be another woman. The primary mentor nourishes your womanhood, helps to bring healing to your emotions, and helps ensure your character is befitting a godly woman. The primary mentor has the greatest impact on your life.

The male mentor is more like a coach. They inspire you to reach your full potential in a specific area in your life, as we see here in our story with Mordecai and Esther. It has been my experience that male mentors are like older brothers and uncles in my life. I also have a relationship with their wives. When receiving counsel or input from them, it's usually in a team setting and like on-the-job training. I have had the opportunity to be a part of a ministry team where I'm the only woman on the team. The evaluation and impartation from the men have helped me reach spiritual maturity and develop my leadership skills. It has been my experience that when safe places are created for instruction and communication, male mentors can be valuable resources.

If Esther had not been open to receive guidance, counsel, and confidential information from her cousin and mentor,

Mordecai, she would not have been mentally, spiritually, or physically in position to expose Haman's plot. And Mordecai would not have had the authority to rewrite the decree if Esther hadn't given him credit for exposing the wicked scheme against the king. (See Esther 8:7–10.) In the end, after Esther exposed Haman's scheme and he was executed, both she and Mordecai were given a remarkable amount of authority in the kingdom.

Jesus has raised us up and set us in positions of leadership, and men can support God's work in us by recognizing, mentoring, and promoting our gifts, talents, and skills.

Satan has put a great divide in male-female relationships in the kingdom, and sin has distorted the relationship between man and woman at every level. But God is restoring the unity in male-female relationships that was lost in the garden. The Lord is giving revelation and insight, causing men and women to understand their different roles in relationship to one another. I believe the Lord is restoring unity, respect, and collaboration in male-female relationships to accomplish His purpose in the earth. The Lord is causing collaboration and teamwork to increase between men and women so that an orphaned generation might be saved from genocide.

This kind of teamwork carries with it the fullness of the nature of God's character. As fathers and mothers who have gained God's mind-set on male-female teamwork nurture sons and daughters, those sons and daughters will then grow up to become fathers and mothers who also nurture sons and daughters with the proper male-female mind-set, creating a godly legacy in the earth.

PRAYER TO ACTIVATE
MALE-FEMALE TEAMWORK

Two are better than one, because they have a good
[more satisfying] reward for their labor; for if they fall,
the one will lift up his fellow. But woe to him who is
alone when he falls and has not another to lift him
up! Again, if two lie down together, then they have
warmth; but how can one be warm alone? And though
a man might prevail against him who is alone, two will
withstand him. A threefold cord is not quickly broken.
                                            —ECCLESIASTES 4:9–12, AMP

*Father, I thank You that You are restoring male
and female relationships in the body of Christ. Your
Word says that two are better than one. I pray for
divine connection and men with a pure heart to be
drawn to me. I loose myself from pains from the past.
Lord, the power of Your blood cleanses my heart
from all bitterness. I will be a woman of authority
and submit to men in authority. I command every
wall of division and suspicion to fall between men
and women in leadership. There is safety in numbers.
I will not be a woman who is isolated and outside
the protection of a team. I choose to trust those in
leadership over me. I am not God's alternative plan.
I am specifically and intentionally called, anointed,
and appointed to fulfill His kingdom purposes in the
earth. In Jesus's name, amen.*

Chapter 10

DESIGNED *for* INFLUENCE

Your eyes saw my substance, being yet unformed. And in
Your book they all were written, the days fashioned for me,
when as yet there were none of them.

—Psalm 139:16

THERE IS A prophetic book over your life. Everybody has
a book in the heavens in which God has already written,
designed, and fashioned your days. We have to take a look
at the blueprint of our lives and get a fresh vision for the
ultimate design and not get caught up in the mundane tasks
of the day. Your days were fashioned for you when there was
yet none of them (Ps. 139:16). But you know how there's an
"insert" button on the computer? The devil is trying to insert
his days into your book. The Lord says that you need to get
that "delete" button and begin to delete the enemy's works
from your life by the Word of God.

Poverty, sickness, and torment from the enemy are not in
your book. Those things are under the curse. They are not
part of the life that God designed for you. Jesus died so you
may have life and life more abundantly.

It is up to you to press into God and ask Him to unlock

the secrets and mysteries in that book. It's up to you whether your life on earth is a pamphlet or a novel. You have the power to decide to live out everything the Lord has written about you in that book. Declare to God that you will do all that He has designed for you to do, that you will press in to find out what those things are.

You see, I am not writing this book about the Esther anointing so that we can go on living without a clue, living outside of our purpose, making no impact on the kingdom whatsoever. No. I am writing because I know that God has called women to go even higher in Him. We are His secret weapon on the earth. And while the enemy may have every intention of keeping us blind and distracted, I know that God has put His mantle on me to be a voice to women in this season.

We are not in this world in this time and season by chance. Every detour and situation in our lives have converged into this very moment. We have come to the kingdom of God for such a time as this. We were put here to prosper. We were put here to display the glory of His kingdom in the earth. We were put here to bring deliverance and healing to our families, our friends, and even strangers we come in contact with. God has formed and fashioned your days. He has designed you to influence people and systems for His glory.

Sure, our stories aren't pretty. We've explored Esther's past—an orphan, a woman, a second-class citizen. But know this: just because trials and tragedies, violation, and shame may have come into your life, it does not mean God has forgotten the plans He has for you. He has not changed His mind about you having dominion and authority to speak and influence the territory He has given you. Don't be moved by what you see happening in the natural. God is aligning things by His Spirit so that you will have favor, boldness, and courage to carry out all that He has commissioned you to do. Look to God to reveal the pages of your book. He is the ultimate designer of your life, not man.

FOUR ANOINTINGS for SUPERNATURAL INFLUENCE

I believe that God has set forth four key anointings to impart to women of God in this season. All four of these anointings will manifest in the lives of modern-day Esthers, and their influence will expand God's kingdom in the earth. These anointings are:

An unshakable love for God that will cause us to love others

In this season God is releasing to women an unshakable love poured out to us from His heart that will enable us to love all people. We are getting ready to experience a surge of revival in our lives, and this will cause an influx of people to come into our lives whom we may have never come in contact with otherwise.

We must let God define what this love looks like. We must set our affections on things above (Col. 3:2). The Holy Spirit will teach us how to love God and how to love one another. Love is not humanistic. You can't love God any way you want to. We must love Him with all our minds, all our hearts, and all our strength. We are coming to a place of affection-based obedience. Jesus said, "If you love Me, keep my commandments" (John 14:15).

This love will cause us to be ready to lay down our lives for others. It's not sloppy agape. True love will break through anything and cause us to see the human in those who have been dehumanized—even those whom we would normally fear and shy away from.

You have the greatest level of influence on somebody when they know you love them. They will trust you to speak into their lives. They will trust you to pray for them. They will trust you with their lives. Think about it. When you know that God loves you, you can have faith. The Bible says that "faith…worketh by love" (Gal. 5:6, KJV). In my own experience when I know God loves me, I believe even more what He says. When you understand how much He loves you and that He will move heaven and earth on your behalf, you will have faith. This is the love that we are designed to display in order to be an influence to those around us.

Supernatural wisdom to influence and disciple nations

> Teach us to number our days, that we may gain a
> heart of wisdom.
> —PSALM 90:12, NIV

The wisdom that I am speaking about here is not the gift of wisdom. The Lord is releasing a supernatural anointing of wisdom, an abiding anointing of wisdom. God will give you supernatural wisdom for the person on your job who loves to come tell you about their problems, or that millionaire in your circle who doesn't know what to do about their schizophrenic child.

You may not be one who preaches messages publicly in the pulpit, but you can preach the best message to someone's life, healing and delivering them through the wisdom of God that flows through you.

This is the same wisdom that Solomon had (1 Kings 4:29). Solomon asked God for supernatural wisdom, and He gave it to him. God will release to you this same anointing for supernatural wisdom. You will know things you aren't supposed to know, things you hadn't even studied. He will give you this wisdom by inspiration. This wisdom allowed Solomon to be a king, an inventor, a songwriter (songs penetrate the human heart). This is the same wisdom that was with God when He created the earth. To the modern-day Esthers, God will give inventions, cures, books, songs, solutions to problems, words of wisdom, and knowledge that has the power to shake nations.

Ask God for this supernatural wisdom. James 1:5–6 says, "If any of you lacks wisdom, let him ask of God, who gives to all liberally and without reproach, and it will be given to him." Why not you; why not now?

We need divine wisdom to rest upon us, to fill us up, and to pour out of our mouths. Through this wisdom we will bring forth the influence we were designed for.

Uncompromising boldness to preach the gospel

I discussed boldness in chapter 7, but I want to point out that this particular anointing for boldness will cause us to preach the gospel without fear or compromise. This boldness is not so that we can boast and promote ourselves. This boldness is not so that we can build our kingdoms. This boldness will give us courage to speak the truth of God's Word wherever we are and to those who need to hear the good news. The Bible says that we have a debt to everybody to preach the gospel to them. (See Romans 1:14–15.)

The gospel is what fills the empty places in people's lives. When we speak the truth of the gospel, we crush the windpipe of the devil who is trying to speak lies to them; the enemy tells them they are nothing, that they're nobody. When we tell people they are fearfully and wonderfully made, we shut the mouth of the enemy. When we preach the gospel to our children who are confused about who they are, we are putting our foot on the enemy's neck and crushing it. This is what it means to tread upon scorpions and serpents. The anointing to boldly preach the gospel of Jesus Christ brings the miraculous power of God into dismal situations and increases the influence of God's kingdom.

An outbreak of the miraculous healings, deliverance, provision, and salvations

The Lord wants to reach people of all nations and bring them to salvation. He is using women who will operate in resurrection power in places where they have been oppressed. We will be a sign and wonder to our oppressors. (See Isaiah 8:18.) In many nations we are considered nonthreatening, so oftentimes the authorities are baffled by women preaching in power and authority so they just leave us alone.

The Lord is empowering women with miraculous power to influence human hearts for the glory of God. He releases miracles to show that He is a loving God who acts on our behalf. Supernatural healing shows God's compassion causing many to turn to Him. In Luke 7:16 when Jesus raised the widow's son from the dead, the people said, "God has come to help his people" (NIV).

The power of the Holy Spirit comes to encourage belief in the one true God and validate the message of the messenger. First Thessalonians 1:5–6 says: "For our gospel did not come to you in word only, but also in power, and in the Holy Spirit and in much assurance, as you know what kind of men we were among you for your sake. And you became followers of us and of the Lord, having received the word in much afflic-tion, with joy of the Holy Spirit."

There are many who may never agree with women being preachers, but they won't be able to deny the hand of the Lord resting upon our lives. God's hand will empower us to accomplish great healings and deliverance on His behalf. There are many women with issues of blood and daughters who are dying that need our healing hands in their lives. We must not get caught by the enticing words of man's wisdom, but we must go forward and manifest the power of God.

YOUR WONDERFUL PLACE

> I will praise You, for I am fearfully and wonderfully made; marvelous are Your works, and that my soul knows very well.
>
> —PSALM 139:14

Woman of God, you are marvelous and wonderful! There is a place in the earth where you can be all that and more. I call this your wonderful place. This is the place that the four anointings I listed above will operate accurately and effectively in the spirit. We've already talked about territory and how each queen has an assigned territory. Consider your wonderful place as your territory. This is a place where you are loved and you feel impassioned to serve here. Your wonderful place is where you are wanted and needed and appreciated.

This does not mean that you will be free from opposition there, but you will have a supernatural grace to overcome. In your wonderful place God has ordained for you, you will be fruitful and will have wisdom to solve conflicts and problems that may arise in that place. You will always have naysayers and haters, but in your wonderful place you will also be supported and appreciated like nowhere else.

There are some places and people who are totally irrelevant to your call and purpose. They are a waste of time and energy. They are a distraction from your core assignment. But in your wonderful place, you will feel a strong sense of purpose, joy, and acceptance.

You know why I go to the nations? Because they think I'm wonderful. They love for me to come and bless them with the Word of the Lord. That is where I know I am valued and appreciated, where I am flowing in an unshakable love for God and others, where I am flowing in the supernatural anointing of wisdom, where I feel unhindered to preach the gospel with boldness, and where the miracles of God are a common occurrence. Sure, there is opposition. The devil always tries to hinder the work of the kingdom. But there is a sense of destiny and fruitfulness that I experience there more than in other places.

Where is your wonderful place? I hope that chapter 7 has you wanting to answer this question more than ever.

Everybody is trying to fit into one mold, but we will not. I am not wonderful where you are wonderful. We each must find that place God designed us to be.

Woman of God, I challenge you to pursue God and ask Him to show you the place where you are wonderful. Ask Him to send you to a people who will think you are wonderful. The church is a training ground—a distribution center. It is not designed to be a place in which everybody can be wonderful. We can't all stay within the four walls, trying to preach, pray, or prophesy to the same people week after week. We are a sent people. We are to be sent out to do a work, rather than staying in the church trying to prove something.

As women we fill so many roles and take up many valuable places in society, yet that religious spirit can try to torment us, saying that we aren't effective unless we are ministers. Everybody is not called to be in the house. Some of us are actually called to the marketplace. Some of us are called to the political realm. God has given us influence, but we have to find that place, and I believe that God has appointed this time for you to find it and be confident in it.

Just as God called Esther out from among her people to be a deliverer and example to women throughout eternity, He has placed His hand on you. You are designed to be a powerful and influential woman for this time. I declare that this is the set time for you to shine brightly and be God's Esther in your family, at your workplace, in your city, and in your nation. You are a queen in the King's court who will rule with grace, wisdom, discernment, and boldness. I declare that your finest hour is upon you. Don't let the devil deceive you. You were designed to carry out the mandates of a heavenly kingdom, a kingdom without end. You were designed to bless the name of the Lord and make His name known. You were designed to walk in prosperity. You were designed to write decrees that reverse the plots of the enemy. You were designed to break the back of poverty, sickness, and disease. You were designed for influence.

PRAYER THAT ACTIVATES
SUPERNATURAL WISDOM

Lord, pour out Your wisdom upon me. Put Your words in my mouth. Let my heart be filled with wisdom. Lord, I release over me now a supernatural anointing of wisdom. Let that supernatural awakening to wisdom come—that supernatural dimension to know things I would not know on my own—to know the when, the how, the why, and the what.

Release to me wisdom to influence nations. Give me that supernatural release of wisdom that the Apostle Paul prayed about. Let dreams and visions begin to churn in my belly. Let thoughts I have never thought before come to me. Wisdom stands at the gate telling me and commanding me to cry out for discernment. God, give me discernment in finances. God, let me begin to understand the economic system as never before.

Open up Your heart to me, Father. I receive Your supernatural anointing for the spirit of wisdom to come into my life. I know that wisdom is one of the sevenfold spirits of the Holy Ghost that

Jesus walked in and caused Him to be able to judge the nations. Release this wisdom to me now in Jesus's name. Amen.

Prayer That Activates a Spirit of Influence

Influence is the capacity to have an effect on the character, development, or behavior of someone or something, or the effect itself. Influence is the power to change or affect someone or something; the power to cause changes without directly forcing them to happen.

Father, I thank You that You are awakening influence inside of me. Awaken me to my sphere of influence. Remove the scales from my eyes that I may see those I've been designed to touch. Lord, You've given me unique gifts and talents to affect those around me. Let the gifts that You've given me make room for me in the earth. Let me have creativity and free expression of my gifts. Let me connect with those who will train and equip me. I will start where I am, while pressing into all that You have for me. I will not draw back in fear. I will impart that which I have to those assigned to my life.

Lord, send me to those who will think I'm wonderful. Send me to those who have an ear to hear my voice.

I decree that I am a change agent. I decree that I have wisdom, insight, and influence with the next generation. I decree that I am aligned for my assignment. I decree that I am fearfully and wonderfully made in Your image. I will find the place where my influence will operate. I will find my wonderful place. In Jesus's name, amen.

NOTES

Introduction
You Were Made *for* More

1. KimberlyDaniels.net, "About Kimberly Daniels," http://kimberlydaniels.net/about-kimberly-daniels/ (accessed July 26, 2014).

Chapter 2
Favor *for* Your Assignment

1. Duane Vander Klok, *Unleashing the Force of Favor* (Grand Rapids, MI: Baker Publishing Group, 2006).

2. For more information, visit www.btlife.org, www.rootscenter.org.

Chapter 3
The Power *of* Your Perfume

1. Roberta Wilson, *Aromatherapy* (New York: Penguin Putnam Inc., 2002), 96–97. Viewed online at Google Books.

2. *Woman's Study Bible* (Nashville: Thomas Nelson, 1997, 1995), s.v. "Esther 2:3."

3. Ray C. Stedman, "Nehemiah: Rebuilding the Walls," http://www.pbc.org/system/message_files/3048/0216.html (accessed July 20, 2014).

4. Robert Jamieson, A. R. Fausset, and David Brown, *A Commentary, Critical, Practical, and Explanatory on the Old and New Testaments* (N.p.: J. B. Names & Company, 1882), http://biblehub.com/commentaries/jfb/nehemiah/2.htm (accessed July 20, 2014).

Chapter 4
Awaken *to* Destiny

1. BrainyQuote.com, "Albert Einstein Quote," http://www
.brainyquote.com/quotes/quotes/a/alberteins165190.html
(accessed July 20, 2014).

Chapter 5

Rule *and* Reign With *the* Scepter

of Prayer *and* Fasting

1. IHOP Tallahassee Missions Base, "The Revelation of Intercession," http://ihoptallahassee.org/documents/teaching-notes/
081310_the-revelation-of-intercession.doc (accessed July 20,
2014).

2. *Webster's Dictionary 1828*, Online Edition, s.v. "territory,"
http://webstersdictionary1828.com/ (accessed July 20, 2014).

Chapter 6

Break Free From *the* Orphan Spirit

1. BrainyQuote.com, "Eleanor Roosevelt Quote," http://
www.brainyquote.com/quotes/quotes/e/eleanorroo127143.html
(accessed July 21, 2014).

2. Yaacov Cohen, "The Tragic Life of Queen Esther," Huff-
ington Post, http://www.huffingtonpost.com/yaacov-cohen/the
-tragic-life-of-queen-esther_b_2722130.html (accessed July 21,
2014).

3. Leland Ryken, *Words of Delight: A Literary Introduction to
the Bible* (Grand Rapids, MI: Baker Books, 1993). Viewed online
at Google Books.

CHAPTER 7
WALK *in* BOLDNESS *and* COURAGE

1. Jack Hayford, executive ed., *New Spirit-Filled Life Bible* (Nashville, TN: Thomas Nelson, 2002), 1497.
2. Ibid.

CHAPTER 8
REWRITE *the* DECREE

1. Jane Hamon, *The Cyrus Decree* (N.p.: Christian International Ministries, 2002).
2. James Strong, *Strong's Exhaustive Concordance of the Bible* (Peabody, MA: Hendrickson Publishers Inc., 2007), 1483.
3. Ibid., 1470.
4. Ibid., 1567.